SPEAKING VOLUMES

SPEAKING VOLUMES
Ken Nordine's *Word Jazz*

GREGORY STEPHENSON

Ober-Limbo Verlag

SPEAKING VOLUMES:
Ken Nordine's *Word Jazz*

Published by Ober-Limbo Verlag
Heidelberg, Germany

ISBN: 978-87-971569-0-2

Cover design and layout:
Birgit Stephenson

For Birgit,
resident genius

"Jazz eludes dogma."

— Preston Whaley Jr.

"World is crazier and more of it than we think."

— Louis MacNeice

For over sixty years, from various exotic non-localities deep in the unmapped interior of his imagination, Ken Nordine (1920-2019) sent back a series of elusively astute, vividly cryptic dispatches in the form of LPs, audio cassettes, CDs, radio broadcasts and a DVD. Nordine's "word jazz," – as he named his self-invented medium of expression – is informed by exuberant invention, whimsical surrealism and quirky humor, but it is also slyly subversive, embracing elements of satire and social critique, as well as more metaphysical musings. In the following notes, I would like to consider certain of the recurrent themes of Nordine's work and the context and characteristics of his art. My efforts to elucidate some of the deeper meanings and broader aims of word jazz are proposed as provisional and exploratory, and are in no way intended as foreclosing other perspectives and possibilities. I make no attempt to cover completely the extensive body of Nordine's work, but have, instead, chosen to focus my attention on the word jazz albums produced between 1957 and 2014 – that is from the earliest to the latest albums – together with a selection of the "Now, Nordine" and "Ken Nordine's Word Jazz" radio shows, and with a quick glance at the word jazz DVD, *The Eye is Never Filled*.

On the front cover of Ken Nordine's first word jazz LP, the album's title – *Word Jazz* – is preceded by the phrase "a somewhat new medium." In the liner notes on the reverse of the album sleeve, we learn that the descriptive phrase on the front cover is that applied by Nordine himself to his work. Nordine's notes then go on to explain something of the origin and the nature of the medium in which he works, locating its primary source in the practice of free association and comparing the imagination when thus engaged to "a jazz instrument wailing words, verbal riffs that swing from images to ideas to images ..." [1] Later, in a pamphlet titled *Publication One,* in a piece titled "A Word About Word Jazz," Nordine offers an explanation that confirms and extends the one set down in the liner notes. Word jazz, Nordine writes here is "a kind of free association ... a dead seriousness with an alive comicness." [2]

It seems to me that there are several points of interest to be pursued in these explanatory statements by Nordine. It is noteworthy that he credits the practice of free association as being the inception of and inspiration for his work. In this sense, then, Nordine's pieces can be seen (in common with surrealism and abstract expressionism) as bringing to conscious expression images and connections from the pre-conscious mind. The author also insists that complementing the wild invention and the comic elements that often characterize his work, there is "a dead seriousness," that is resonance with and significance in relation to life's multiple meanings. Also of import in Nordine's explanation of the medium of word jazz is his likening of the imagination to a musical instrument employed in creating jazz, an instrument giving free rein to invention. His works, then, may be seen as a counterpart to the improvisational solo of a jazz musician, taking their point of departure in a recognizable conceptual referent, then pulling away from it, exploring its structural components and its implications.

What Nordine seems to aim for in performing word jazz is a kind of perceptual and conceptual syncopation, something off-beat, off-center, an intellectual shift of accent, a deviation from the regular, expected patterns of thought. In the spirit of jazz, the medium of word jazz offers "improvisational freedom and structural openness." [3] With the opportunities afforded by such freedom, Nordine takes the given, the conventional, the truism and the platitude, turning them inside out and upside down. In so doing, he calls attention to the limitations of accepted boundaries and definitions, rigid categories and single-minded standards, and implicitly proposes, instead, a wider, wilder perspective on the mystery of existence.

In its essentials, a word jazz composition consists of spoken words, jazz accompaniment and sound effects. The words most often take the form of a monologue, a narrative or a playlet (two voices in dialogue). The narratives are related from a first person or third person point-of-view. The jazz music introduces the individual performances or texts, and also serves to evoke or enhance mood or to underscore action during the course of the piece. The sound effects act both as objects of attention and comment in themselves (as in "The Sound Museum") or as illustrations of the narrative (the ticking clocks in "What Time is It?"). The most immediate and obvious precursor to Nordine's word jazz performances is radio drama of the kind broadcast over radio networks from the 1930s through the 1950s. Such dramas, which included soap operas, thrillers, mysteries and comedies, employed similar techniques (i.e. words, music, sound effects). While clearly allied to this type of drama, Nordine's word jazz compositions are distinguished from their predecessors by their unconventional character: their unwonted topics, their atypical protagonists, their idiosyncratic themes, their jazz-inspired ethos. By the latter quality, I mean that in common with jazz, Nordine's work is eclectic, protean, innovative, unpredictable, and ultimately "defies attempts to fix its uses, parameters, qualities and meanings." [4] In this regard, it is perhaps worth mentioning what Robert S. Gold has described as "the jazzman's fondness for the bizarre, eccentric or unconventional." [5] The jazzman's affinity for such qualities is, as Gold notes, often expressed in the terms of approbation employed in the jazz milieu, including "crazy," "nutty," "insane," "mad," "way-out," "far-out," and "gone," any or all of which might suitably be applied to Ken Nordine's word jazz.

Although it is in many instances assuredly true that "it ain't what you say, it's the way that you say it," with regard to word jazz, both the "what" and the "way" are vital and complementary components, working together to elicit in the imagination of the listener an invisible theatre of the mind. Ken Nordine's considerable vocal skills – acquired and honed through his professional work as a radio announcer and commercial voice-over artist – are founded on his resonant baritone voice and enhanced by his effective use of pace, pitch, articulation, pauses and emphases. Nordine deploys to maximum effect what Jeff Porter has called "the incantatory power of voice." [6] It is the deft modulations of his disembodied voice reaching us through speakers or earphones that engage our imagination as listeners, evoking in our minds characters, situations and settings. As Donald McWhinnie observed in his book *The Art of Radio,* "every listener must translate the sound-pattern he hears into his own mental language; he must apply his imagination to it and transform it." [7] In this manner, as listeners we become active collaborators in Nordine's world of word jazz.

In its own highly individual and idiosyncratic way, Nordine's work can be seen to belong to the phonographic genre of spoken word recordings. Poetic recitations and readings by authors or actors go back to the very earliest days of the phonograph industry, beginning to increase in appeal among some purchasers of records during the late 1930s and early 1940s with Orson Welles' renderings of Shakespeare's plays and Charles Laughton's renderings of G.B. Shaw and other authors. The Caedmon LP of the Welsh poet Dylan Thomas reading his poetry and prose, (*Selections from the Writings of Dylan Thomas Read by the*

Poet, TC 1002) issued in 1952, was a modest milestone in "high culture spoken word" recordings, its relative popularity revealing a market for "niche or narrowcast" media products. [8] In the wake of the unexpectedly favorable and even profitable reception of recordings by Dylan Thomas and other contemporary poets, some few years later, other small, independent record companies and even major record companies began to market spoken word LPs with an even narrower market in mind, that is that of adherents of the hip subculture of the mid Fifties (a topic to which I will shortly return). Early examples of such discs are Lord Buckley's *Hipsters, Flipsters and Finger Poppin' Daddies Knock Me Your Lobes* (RCA Victor LPM-3246) issued in 1955, and *Poetry Readings in the Cellar* by Kenneth Rexroth and Lawrence Ferlinghetti (Fantasy 7002) issued in 1957. These were later followed by LP readings (some with musical accompaniment) by Beat Generation authors, Jack Kerouac, Allen Ginsberg and others, as well as hip comedy LPs by Shorty Petterstein (Henry Jacobs), Mort Sahl, Lenny Bruce and Del Close.

It is into this latter cultural environment, this subcultural subset, that Ken Nordine's *Word Jazz* LP makes its distinctive entrance. [9] The Nordine disc is, in fact, among the earliest such hip culture (as distinct from high culture) spoken word

LPs, having been recorded and released by Dot Records in 1957, as part of their "Jazz Horizons" series. What hip was (or is) and what was (or is) hip can be, of course, contested questions, *fraught,* as they say, *with imminent peril.* On the authority of Tom Dalzell, a recognized expert in the study of slang, the term hip (or hep) is said to go back to the early decades of the 20th century, and was used then and thereafter to mean "aware, world-wise, sophisticated and up-to-date with trends in music, fashion and speech." [10] Others have pointed to the essential elusiveness of the concept expressed by the word: "Hip is hard to nail ... an uncrackable code," write Roy Carr, Brian Case and Fred Dellar in their monograph titled *The Hip;* it is an attitude, a stance that eschews and evades "manifestos ...majorities and fashions." [11] The state of being hip – hipness – may, according to Steven Brown Goldberg, a sociologist of popular culture, be most accurately understood as "sophistication" or "awareness," to which he adds that hipness also implies "a certain amount of alienation." [12] Phil Ford, a professor of music, extends and deepens these dimensions of the meaning of hip, proposing a concept that he designates "hip sensibility." [13] According to Ford, "hipness is a state of mind. It is a sensibility and aesthetic," driven by "the individual's alienation from society – alienation that is due not to any specific political wrong but to something more radical, a clash of sensibility and perception." [14] Hipness implies, then, an oblique, individual perspective on the world, on existence and on society and its associated phenomena. Or, as John Leland observes in his extended treatment of the topic: "Hip is an ethos of individualism." [15] Examining postwar hip culture, the scholar, Alisa White, rightly identifies a concurrence in the 1950s and 1960s of several hip subcultures, "including jazz musicians, black and white hipsters, and the beats." [16] White further notes that: "While the hip styles of these subcultures varied, they all emphasized individuality, nonconformity, spontaneity, authenticity, and direct unmediated self-expression." [17] The various qualities specified above are, of course, easily to be seen in Nordine's quirky *Word Jazz*, allying Nordine's art with the freewheeling, idiosyncratic spirit of hip and situating it within the context of the nascent underground cultural rebellion of the 1950s, the ferment stirring beneath the surface of mass entertainment, consumerism and consensus in the postwar period.

Hip culture, then, may be said to define itself in opposition or resistance to the mainstream or the prevailing, the established, the conventional, against both high culture and mass culture. In the United States, in the affluent post war period, social commentators such as William F. Whyte and

David Riesman pointed with alarm to what they perceived to be a drift toward materialism and consumerism, toward incipient standardization, homogeneity, conformity and complacent consensus. The growth of large organizations, corporations and institutions, together with the spread of mass media and the advent of mass production and mass marketing, were regarded by Whyte, Riesman and others as detrimental to the integrity of the individual self and the human spirit. As against the mass and the mainstream, hip culture can be seen to embody a minor, marginal divergent-insurgent countertrend, with hipness proposing an alternative ideal or identity to that of *The Organization Man, The Man in the Gray Flannel Suit,* or life as an anonymous member of *The Lonely Crowd.* [18] The antithesis of hip and hipness was, of course, the inhibited inhabitant of squaresville, the archetypal (reductive perhaps mythical) square who was seen as the embodiment of all that was conventional, complacent, materialistic, status-seeking, unaware, unreflective, unquestioning, repressed, narrow, shallow and inauthentic. These issues, these tensions, so germane to postwar American culture, find expression as themes in Ken Nordine's *Word Jazz,* where they are often treated in a nuanced and equitable fashion, for finally the most authentic hipness is to be found in the ability to interrogate and discriminate freely, independently and for oneself, in preserving what Phil Ford calls "the sovereignty of the individual intellect." [19]

Even when considered in the context of hip culture spoken word LPs, Ken Nordine's *Word Jazz* is quite unlike anything else in that category. The tracks on the *Word Jazz* LPs consist of stories and short plays (such as "The Vidiot") in which Nordine's central concern may be said to be the nature of reality, including the nature of the self and the nature of society. An obvious and useful place to begin a consideration of Nordine's inquiry into these themes would be with the first track on the first **Word Jazz** LP, a composition titled "What Time Is It?"

This is a tale of psychological awakening and transformation, but one in which the optimism implicit in such a theme is slyly qualified. At the outset of the narrative, the nameless and nondescript protagonist exhibits every characteristic of the archetypal "square." His life, we are told, is conducted in a strictly "regular" manner, his routine inflexible and banal in every detail. There is in everything he does a suffocating sameness. The catalyst for his transformation comes in the form of a practical joke perpetrated upon him by a friend. Every night at 2 a.m. the friend phones "this regular liver," whispering to him over the phone the same question: "what time is it?" So inclined to habit and routine is the protagonist that when the practical joker ceases to call him at that early hour, in order to sleep the protagonist is now obliged to address the same question to himself, whispering aloud the words: "what time is it?" This accommodation serves the protagonist for a time, but like a delayed reaction explosive device the practical joker's act of disruption serves at length to arouse in the protagonist's mind a potent reaction: he begins to question, he begins to wonder. No longer content to reassure himself with local time, he begins to think in terms of global time, then extends his newly stimulated curiosity to sidereal time, to time elsewhere in the universe. He reads about time and buys numerous clocks, all set to different time zones. Clearly, he is now obsessed with time but his obsession has served to expand his awareness, his knowledge, his perspective on existence. His life is no longer banal and unreflective but filled instead with mystery and wonder.

A further unfolding of latent mental ability in the protagonist occurs when – as the result of a minor electrical failure in his home – he discovers that in some inexplicable fashion, without the aid of any apparatus or instrument, he knows the time. This extraordinary new talent, verified by testing, is, however, soon put to a purely prosaic and utilitarian end: serving – in accordance with budget-cutting measure by a new political administration – to replace other time-keeping devices and employees at a government bureau of standards. Not only does this represent a pedestrian appropriation of an exceptional ability, but the protagonist's life is now reduced to one of monotony and confinement. We are told that "he sits in a little room in Washington," (both day and night, presumably) merely telling the time. This can hardly be said to represent much of an improvement upon his former life of routine and repetition. As Jeff Porter remarks of the tale's ending: "The gift of knowing thus becomes an affliction ... Nordine's timekeeper cannot escape the absurd, locked in a small room indefinitely. There is for him no exit."[20]

This wry tale seems a kind of parable of the complexities of psychological liberation. The tale would seem to propose that there are within the human psyche urges and energies seeking experience beyond the normal physical level of existence, but that there are also – both within and without – powerful forces striving to contain, constrain and thwart the expression of such urges. Just as new levels of conscious awareness are available and can be attained, Nordine suggests, so too can they be misappropriated, diverted, vitiated. Liberation (radical psychological development) is not as simple and straightforward a process as we might hope or as some would believe.

A similar appetite for transformation or transcendence and the frustration of that appetite are treated in another of the LP's tracks, titled "The Flibberty Jib on the Bippity Bop." The narrator here has been a witness to and a participant in the events he relates. Another equivocal parable-like tale, this story concerns the attainment and loss (twice) by a community of a cherished collective experience of transporting ecstasy. The catalyst for their sudden ascent to a heightened level of consciousness is a mysterious stranger who arrives in their town and invites them all to a gathering in the auditorium where by means of a rhythmic chant, he lifts them out of their sole selves and their humdrum lives into a state of rapture. Faith in this potent stranger is, however, undermined by certain elements in the community, "critics" who envy the stranger's power and popularity, and the ecstatic gatherings he conducts soon come to an end. In consequence of the machinations of the "critics," the stranger loses his power, leaving town in despair and defeat, while the community returns to its banal routine, its dullness and blandness. Gray, hopeless years pass and then – against all expectation – the same chain of events is again enacted, a charismatic stranger arrives in town and by means of the same chant or mantra induces in his receptive audience a condition of ecstasy, whereafter inevitably the local "critics" again succeed in undercutting the stranger's mysterious power and in driving him from town, a man demoralized and overcome by self-doubt.

The central, essential and fundamental premise on which the tale is constructed is that of an intense desire latent among ordinary people for ecstatic transcendence. The mysterious strangers and their shared nonsense mantra merely serve as vehicles for the realization of this desire. But in raising the community to exaltation, what is the motive of these strangers? The twin mystagogues of the tale seem to veer dangerously close to being demagogues. Does their dramatic dynamism cloak opportunistic egocentricity? Or are they, in fact, genuine prophets and deliverers? And what of those referred to as "the critics?" We are told that their motive is envy, yet if the mysterious strangers are, indeed, potential demagogues, seducing the community for reasons of personal power, then the objectives of the critics in maligning the strangers are worthy though their motive for doing so is corrupt. Nordine's strange tale seems to be more on the order of an inquiry into these issues rather than an attempt to offer any definitive judgements upon them.

In the end, we are left with the continuing tension between existence as banality and futility (imaged in the tale as darkness) and the possibility of ecstatic deliverance (imaged as light). And we are left, too, with the narrator's concluding question: "By the way, how are things in your town?" Even this question seems somewhat ambiguous and curiously haunting. Is it merely a casual, conversational query? Does it implicitly suggest that we ought to consider in what manner these issues manifest themselves in the lives we live? Or is the tone of the question (as it seems to me to be) one of forlorn yearning, of anxious, wistful hope that elsewhere there may be found a new and true deliverer?

Transporting power – at least to some degree – may also be manifest in certain works of art, as exemplified in "The Sound Museum." This track presents to the listener a series of "sound paintings," brief abstract soundscapes rich in poetic suggestion. Each sound painting transports the listener to another world or dimension, visionary or infernal. Compelling, surprising, disturbing, mysterious, challenging conventional notions of what constitutes art, the sound paintings are the antithesis of the ordinary, the accustomed and the predictable. (A perceptive reading of "The Sound Museum" in relation to the hip sensibility is to be found in Phil Ford's excellent article: "Hip Sensibility in an Age of Mass Counterculture.") [21]

On other tracks on the *Word Jazz* LP, Nordine depicts individual lives cramped by convention, desperately dependent upon diversion, arrested by their own vanity, trapped in inauthentic identities. In "Looks Like It's Going to Rain," a first person narrator acknowledges the marked contrast between his outward, social behaviour and his actual inner state. He recognizes that he is living "a lie." Striving to appear to others casual and calm, making banal observations about the weather, inwardly he feels confused, distressed, fearful, struggling to resist panic. He attempts to find a place of refuge within his mind, reassuring himself by contemplating the logical progression and predictable solidity of numbers, only to have his thoughts lead – inevitably, involuntarily – to the concept of zero: "nothing, no thing, no me, no you, no world." In confrontation with this utter and ultimate lack of meaning, he recoils, returning with some relief to the realm of polite conversational banality. Retracting, in effect, his earlier insight deploring the trivial platitudes of the quotidian world ("nothing's accomplished by this"), in the end he resumes his external, social role, takes up again his mask, dissembles his doubts and fear behind his accustomed disguise.

In a manner similar to that of the narrator of "Looks Like It's Going to Rain," who seeks refuge from ontological insecurity in the comforting regularity of the number system, the epynomous figure of "The Vidiot" attempts to flee from the anxieties that beset him into a universe of endless, mindless diversion as offered by television. This track takes the form of a radio interview between a therapist and his client, with hesitations, interruptions, repetitions and overlapping speech lending verisimilitude to the pastiche (patterned on sober, uncomprehending interviews with heroin addicts.) The self-confessed "vidiot" being interviewed is "hooked" on watching television, currently spending 15 hours a day of viewing, sleeping only a few hours, working only a few hours, sometimes unable to work at all due to his addiction. His chronic need for television, we are told, is based on his need to forget his "troubles and worries." Not only has this behavioral addiction led to a life of isolation and dependency, a life of significantly diminished inner content, a life in which he is driven to break the law by being obliged to have a television set with him in his automobile, but paradoxically his compulsive television viewing has not freed him from anxiety but has, instead, become the focus of a new deeply disturbing anxiety: he worries that he watches too much television. So dependent upon viewing television has he become that the interview is ended abruptly when the "vidiot" experiences the pains of withdrawal, desperately pleading with the therapist for just a few seconds of video input to assuage his distress and discomfort. Following the precipitate departure of his client, the therapist, alone and shaken by the appalling spectacle he has just witnessed and feeling burdened by the responsibilities of his profession, succumbs to the temptation to find a few moments of solace in the entertainment available on television. His enraptured response to the mundane program he views on the screen would seem to indicate that he, too, is soon destined to become addicted to watching television, unwittingly transformed – as if by psychic contamination by his client – into another "vidiot."

"The Vidiot" is a satirical comment both on the insidious inanity of television and on the human tendency to seek avenues of distraction from the essential existential issues of human life, rather than engaging with them. In the course of the sketch, we witness the ease with which individuals can succumb to the seductions of diversion and how readily they can become addicted to shallow distraction, ultimately foreclosing by such evasions the whole human struggle for value and purpose in life.

Another form of distraction from deeper awareness or growth toward fullness of being resides in the temptations of vanity, as dramatized by Nordine in "Roger." This track unfolds in the form of a candid, confessional, first person narrative, wherein the narrator relates a dismaying and fateful event that occurred during his adolescence. At the outset, the narrator comments on deception and self-deception, later developed as the central motifs of the tale. The narrator recalls his teenage ambition to become "a great concert violinist," and his determined work toward that end. At the same time, he now recognizes that this ambition was instilled in him by his friend, Roger, himself a musical prodigy. Roger is dominating, duplicitous, self-aggrandizing and manipulative, alternately humiliating and flattering the narrator. The climactic moment of the tale is the revelation that through some ominous anomaly Roger's teeth betray his true nature, that of a poisonous, predatory creature.

This revelation (prefigured earlier in the tale) is expressed in imagery associated with serpents. Roger, we are told, "slithers" across the living room to the piano, passing a "potted adder's tongue" plant, and moving through "undulating" sunshine. Only then does the narrator perceive his friend's apparently fang-like teeth. The effect of this discovery upon the narrator is to cause him abruptly to put his violin back in its case and leave the house. Profoundly disturbed by what he has seen, the narrator decides that he is "through with music." He has seen through Roger's false friendship, his self-serving flattery, his musical snobbery and vainglory, and understood also the hollowness of his own ambitions. He has perceived that what lies beneath such vanities is cold-blooded reptilian egoism.

The narrator unsparingly depicts himself as having been susceptible to the kind of overweening ambition embodied in Roger (whom he idolized as being "the greatest thing that had happened to the piano since Walter Gieseking"). In a grandiose fantasy prompted by Roger's cunning flattery, the narrator imagined musical achievements as important in their way as the Gettysburg Address, winning for him acclamation, adoration, power. In his fantasy, others (including Roger) are no more than instruments for his lofty validation and veneration, Roger merely an accompanist to the narrator's magnificent performance, the audience no more than "hushed cabbage heads." The subsequent startling, unsettling disclosure of Roger's true nature is a decisive moment in the narrator's young life. Renouncing ambition, he suddenly becomes alert to other forms of endeavor in the world around him: noticing (with interest and apparently for the first time) on his path homeward the sidewalk stamp and wondering about the goals and ambitions of the cement contractor whose name is imprinted in the sidewalk.

Word Jazz is an inventive, distinctive contribution to the hip sensibility of the 1950s. Against the prosaic, the static, the bland and the mundane, Nordine proposes quirky humor and a sense of mystery. In "the age of television" and ubiquitous, intrusive advertising displays, Nordine affirms the primacy of the oral, the intimate and the individual in human communication. The album introduces several themes and devices that will become characteristic of Nordine's subsequent work. These include protagonists who are somewhat neurotic, anxious, self-conscious and introspective, protagonists who are subject to sudden obsessions, who feel secret desperation, who seek to liberate themselves from confined lives, who ponder particulars ranging from cracks and cement contractor stamps in the sidewalks to the origins of the numerical system and time on Arcturus, protagonists who sometimes succumb to self-deception and forms of banal escapism, and who are sometimes ambushed by awe. The motifs of time, social criticism, numbers, the ambiguity and opacity of the world and the human heart, and the quest for some form of "beyondness" or transcendence are also recurrent in later *Word Jazz* albums. Characteristic, too, of Nordine's later work are the whimsical and poetical touches that occur in the course of these early *Word Jazz* narratives, details such as egg timers given as gifts to friends in

"What Time Is It?," interjections such as the phrase "upper limbo" in the track titled "My Baby," the pretentious French pronunciation of the name "James Cunningham" by the curator of "The Sound Museum," or the use of arresting similes such as that likening Roger moving through the sunlit dust motes to "a Brownian movement toward madness." (I am very grateful to Larry Beckett for correcting my mishearing of this phrase and for explaining to me the meaning of Brownian movement: the random motion of particles suspended in a fluid.)

Beneath its wild invention, its wit and whimsy, Ken Nordine's second album, titled *Son of Word Jazz,* consists in the main of tracks expressive of a rather dark view both of the contemporary condition and of the human situation in general. [22] The first track on the LP, "The Smith Family," sets the mood. In this cheerfully bleak parable of the nature of life, an ant named Smith fears and envies a fly named Smith, rejoicing in the fly's death when it is killed by a human hand. The ant's celebration is, however, short-lived as he himself is quickly dispatched, unintentionally and obliviously stepped on by the foot of same fly-killer (and former savior of the ant), a man named Smith. Significantly, none of these Smiths is aware that their rivals, enemies or victims share their surname. Clearly, too, the shared surname suggests an essential inter-relatedness and interdependence of all living creatures, a kinship to be cherished, but one which is, instead, rendered invalid by mutual animosity, envy and indifference.

The destructive proclivities of humanity are an implicit theme of the track titled "Outer Space." This cut takes the form of an historic, inaugural dialogue via interstellar radio between a representative of earth and a member of a distant extraterrestrial civilization. Reversing the familiar science-fiction trope of dangerous aliens, the track proposes that – with our hydrogen bombs and our violent instincts – it is we ourselves who are the dangerous aliens. Further evidence for a latent calamitous human hubris is presented in "Bubble Gum," a monologue spoken by an adult bubble gum fancier. All seems innocent of harm in his seemingly benign obsession with blowing large bubble gum bubbles until the track ends with the sound of a powerful bomb-like explosion. The status-enhancing quest to achieve bigger and bigger gum bubbles ends in tragic self-destruction. It may be that this track is intended as a kind of parable of the arms race. In any case, this brief drama seems to suggest that in small things as well as large things, "pride goeth before destruction." [23]

"The Bullfighter" locates within the human mind a dark desire to destroy, a compulsion seen here as closely allied with vanity. A would-be matador confesses that in order to attain his much-anticipated "moment of truth" in facing and slaying a bull, he must first slay the bull within: "kill the bull inside me." A dark drive toward self-annihilation is also treated in "Lemming." In this monologue, an earnest, perplexed seeker is drawn on in his quest for direction in the world by a mysterious sound: "leading me on but I don't know where it is taking me." At length, a feeling grows within him – even as the night around him grows ever darker – a sense that he is getting closer to the source of the beckoning call. Pursuing the alluring sound, drawn onward by its growing power, he suddenly falls into water and drowns. Lemmings are, of course, legendary for their self-destructive migrations, and are said sometimes to leap to their deaths. The anthropomorphized lemming of this track would seem to represent humanity, drawn unconsciously and inexorably toward self-annihilation.

Another manifestation of an obsessive self-destructive urge is presented in "I Used to Think my Right Hand was Uglier than my Left." In this monologue a man relates his long-standing animus toward his own right hand, detailing the many punishments he has contrived to inflict upon that hapless appendage. A note of hope, however, occurs at the end of the track when the narrator declares that he has now overcome this destructive compulsion.

The tracks "Secretary" and "Anytime, Anytime" dramatize human self-centeredness and lack of empathy. In the former, a contrite boss seeks forgiveness from and reconciliation with his secretary who patently ignores him continuing to type during the whole of his extended apology. In the latter track, which takes place in a bar, we overhear a sad, weary man, near despair, unrolling a long catalog of sorrows and woes, as all the while his female interlocutor responds with helpless laughter, at length imploring him: "stop it, you're killing me." The incongruity of their exchange is potently puzzling. Is she so richly amused because he is such a cliché? Is he so self-involved, so self-absorbed that he is oblivious of the effect upon her of his lamentations? How can two persons who speak the same language fail so utterly to convey meaning or to evoke understanding in the other? On both of these curious tracks there is a sad sense of human isolation, a sense of each figure as enclosed in an invisible prison of vanity or self-pity, each alienated from his fellows, unable to achieve meaningful contact or true communication.

Nor is there much consolation to be found in the transformations of the given world, the world as it is, as undertaken by the protagonists of "Miss Cone" and "Looking at Numbers." In the former track, which takes place in a geometric universe, the narrator, a self-described and literal "square," inspired by feelings of love for "Miss Cone," exercises utmost will and determination in order to transform himself into a three-dimensional entity, hoping in this manner to inspire Miss Cone's interest. Alas, despite his heroic efforts, he is rejected by the object of his affections in favor of a rival, a mere point, a virtual non-entity, possessing zero dimensionality. In "Looking at Numbers," the narrator – through the power of the imagination – transforms numerical digits one through nine into dramatic vignettes, objects, events, prospects. But even the magically transformed poetic world that the narrator of this track creates out of the raw abstract realm of numbers, is flawed and unharmonious; sickness, debasement, hostility and resentment are still to be found there. Beneath the humor and invention of both of these tracks, there is an underlying current of disappointment and failure. Hope and desire and the powers of the human creative imagination are seen ultimately to break up against the obdurate solidity of the Real.

More successful in this regard, but still critically lacking permanence is the utopia created in the imagination of the narrator of "Down the Drain." The protagonist here is a refugee from the pressures of the modern world who seeks solace in solitary warm baths and in a fantasy of sliding down the drain of the bathtub and emerging onto the sunlit shore of one of the Virgin Islands. In this imagined tropical paradise there is no pretence, no competition, no status seeking, only contentment, everyone is self-accepting and accepting of others. The illusion cannot, however, long be sustained, before you are drawn back to the cold, hard world from which you have fled. Once again, on this track, the creative imagination is seen to provide consolation and a kind of compensation for the harshness of the Real World, but such escape as it affords is seen to be only temporary. (I am reminded here of John Keats' "Ode to a Nightingale" where the poet-speaker's spirit takes flight to "faery lands" on the invisible wings of "poesy," but is soon unwillingly returned again to "the weariness, the fever, and the fret" of the physical world.) Nevertheless, the escapist fantasy indulged in by the protagonist of this track affirms the abiding human intuition of another mode of being, a timeless, innocent state, a lost paradise.

A prophecy of full and final deliverance from the fallen world we inhabit is proclaimed in the metaphorically dense, image-rich, poetic piece titled "The Junkman," appropriately the final track on the LP. This sound-text is addressed to a silent companion who inspires love in the speaker of the text and from whom the speaker draws courage. The opening lines establish that although the events recounted took place in a dream while the narrator was sleeping, the dream was "no dream," the sleep "no sleep," in that the experiences and insights of the dream comprise a revelation, a vision of things as they truly are and as they will be.

The setting of the dream-vision is a junkyard, the domain of "the junkman." Here all is broken, rusted, bent, twisted, damaged, spoiled. It becomes clear that the junkman is a parasitic, satanic figure, one who profits from human failure and loss.

His "jungle of jumble" is a realm where the useless refuse he gleefully purchases represents the wreckage of human lives, "lost courage ... odd shaped fears." The narrator – himself spiritually or psychologically damaged, his mind "a rusting headpiece where all metals turn inward" – is at first half receptive to the ranting arguments of the junkman, transfixed by "the wag of his broken jaw" as the junkman's words resonate in his head.

Ultimately, however, the narrator resists the dark logic of the junkman, drawing resolution from contact with his beloved companion, and countering the insidious, reductive reasoning of "the king of unkindness" with a prophecy of redemption. The junkman, he proclaims, will be overturned, diminished to a forgotten figure in an unremembered dream, the junkyard – through love, through courage and caring – restored to a garden. Though we now live in darkness and dispossession, the morning of reclamation and restitution is seen to be at hand.

As a sound-text, an oral poem, "The Junk Man" is comprised of paired, opposing images. The broken, fractured objects enumerated throughout will, we are told, in time future be mended. The "awful laughter" of the junk man will then be superseded by the joyful laughter of generations to come. The junkman's words, likened to "crippled wings," will be replaced by "other wings" fully capable of "flight." Our current disinherited state will be supplanted by recovery of our true inheritance, just as the false "devalued" values of the junk man will be replaced by true human values and virtues. The reign of "unkindness," of which the junkman is dark monarch, will be overthrown by love; the nightmare of now will be resolved in a future awakening; and the night of waste, fear, loss and grief will be displaced by a dawn of deliverance that is, according to the narrator, even now approaching: "Look! The gray twilight of morning creases the edge of the east. It's almost time to wake up."

Implicitly, *Son of Word Jazz* advances an argument. The separate monologues and dialogues of individual tracks together comprise a comprehensive and coherent statement concerning human character: vain, violent, impercipient, wounded, confounded, self-hating, self-pitying, sadly lacking in empathy, close confined in status hierarchies and dull routines. Our condition seems to offer but few consolations (imagination in "Down the Drain"), few instances of successful self-transformation ("I Used to Think …"). Yet the LP culminates in a powerful affirmation of the promise of human love in overcoming isolation and desolation, a revelatory vision of renewal and redemption. In "The Junkman," the dark diagnosis of the earlier tracks is resolved in a prophecy of recovery, an optimistic prognosis of ultimate remedy for our shared spiritual disorder.

An appropriate place from which to begin a consideration of Ken Nordine's third word jazz LP, titled *Next,* might be with the liner notes on the reverse of the album sleeve. [24] Here, there is a text by Nordine, which takes the form of an imaginary interview between a critic or journalist and the artist himself. The title of the piece is "Dialogue between ! and ?" The interviewer poses a series of reductive, sceptical questions, to which Nordine replies in an oblique, poetic fashion. The interviewer clearly wishes to impose meaning on Nordine's LP, even to minimize or resist meaning, while Nordine seeks to preserve mystery, nuance, subtlety and the interplay of multiple meanings. The conflict underlying their conversation is essentially that between fixed principles, pre-established categories and closed systems as against ambiguity and plurality of meaning. (Between, we may say, square and hip worldviews.) An example of Nordine's deft deployment of poetic equivocation occurs in an exchange when with an undertone of condescension the interviewer asks: "What do you possibly hope to accomplish with what you've been doing?" Nordine replies: "Sanction." The word sanction is an auto-antonym or contronym, a word that evokes contradictory or reverse meanings. Sanction can be understood to mean permission, approval, to confirm or allow, but it can also be understood to mean to restrict or to penalize. Which signification of the word is the intended one here? Or, in some paradoxical fashion transcending conventional linguistic logic might both meanings be implied? In brief, I think that the "interview" text serves as a kind of preface to the sound-texts on the album, alerting the listener that restrictive categories and preconceptions are impediments to the discovery of deeper, more complex truths. The wonder, the affirmation, the joy of discovery emblematized by the exclamation point in the title of the interview – "Dialogue between ! and ?" – must be preserved against attrition from the abrasive cynicism and disposition to incredulity so often inherent in the question mark. The text reminds us that it is always easier to classify, to affix a label, to distrust, to disbelieve and dismiss than to attempt to understand.

A recurrent motif among the tracks on *Next* is the urgent attempt by individuals to affix a label to themselves, as it were, to assert an external, social identity, to define themselves in the eyes of others, to secure a foothold in the status hierarchy. This is evident already on the first track of the album, "Mr. Big," in which voices (two male, one female) insistently proclaim their stereotypical masculinity or femininity, pathetically vying for recognition and admiration. The theme is picked up in the next track, titled "Smerd." Here, the listener overhears a political campaign speech delivered at a small town rally by a candidate for office, named Smerd. (The single surname by which he repeatedly refers to himself suggests a truncated identity.) Holding forth in the inflated manner of old style oratory, the self-important Smerd assails his audience with a blizzard of clichés and bombast, barrages of grandiloquent phrases and double-talk. He ends by merely repeating his name, again and again, clearly savouring the sound of it. (It is, indeed, rather an unattractive name, reminiscent of the French word "merde" or excrement. In Dostoyevsky's celebrated novel, *The Brothers Karamazov,* there is an unpleasant character named Smerdyakov, whose name literally means "son of the stinking one." The Russian word for stinking is *smerdiashchaia.*) Grasping desperately after distinction and approval, Smerd inadvertently reveals his essential hollowness and smallness of spirit.

Similarly, the as yet unsuccessful but perennially optimistic inventor-entrepreneur who narrates "Bury-It-Yourself Time Capsules," assumes in his potential customers an appetite for attention and status. His ant-colony picture windows, complete with flashing neon sign, are clearly calculated to confer instant individuality and prestige upon the purchaser. Likewise, his 98 cent Bury-It-Yourself Time Capsules are intended to satisfy a need for personal post-mortem affirmation, promising a kind of ego-immortality as one's most inconsequential private data and opinions are inflicted on generations yet unborn. In parallel with Smerd's unworthy worldly ambitions, the narrator speaks candidly of his own mercenary motives: "I'm always trying to figure out ways to make money ... money's a pretty big thing in our society ... gotta have it." In the mind of the narrator, it would seem, only sufficient capital can endow one with authentic identity.

An urgent quest for self-definition also informs the track titled "Faces in the Jazzmatazz," in which the leit motif of "faces" expresses the various types of identity for which various individuals strive or behind which they hide. The narrator describes pessimistic hedonists and eager seekers of in-group status, together with apparent innocents "looking with the look that little children have," – all chasing some gaudy dream, some phantom of hope or "renaissance," all vainly swimming against the current of time, the tick tock of passing minutes, the inevitable coming of midnight. A short end-rhymed poem, consisting of two couplets, concludes the narrative. This short coda to the track places in perspective all the revellers, celebrants, nihilists, fugitives and questers of the urban jazz night, all of whom will ultimately be obliged to face with their faces "Mr. Must," or death.

The liner notes of *Next* describe the track titled "A Whistler" as treating an instance of "whistling for love in this whistling dark." This characterization of the theme of "A Whistler" resonates with the recurrent theme of self-definition or self-labelling encountered in the foregoing tracks of the album. In this instance, the narrator relates how as a young man he became an accomplished whistler, hoping to achieve recognition and distinction for this talent. Ostentatiously whistling classical music as he walked the streets, he wished to be seen by others as someone special, but was, instead, ignored. In response to this disappointment, he then changed his whistling repertoire to popular tunes and having done so was rewarded by the approval of others. He now whistles, he admits, "like everybody else does," – a total surrender to collective thinking. We see, again, the urgency with which lonely, isolated individuals strive for acceptance by others, often at the price of social conformity with its necessary suppression of the person one truly is or might become. And we sense, again, in the underlying idiom referred to in the liner notes and implicit in "A Whistler," (i.e. *whistling in the dark*, which means an attempt to resist overwhelming fear in frightening circumstances) the existential loneliness of human lives, the desperate human need for identity and meaning in the howling darkness of this world. Unfortunately, this same loneliness and need can drive individuals to self-surrender or futile self-assertion, to acquiesce in adopting shallow social roles or to seek the shelter of seeming certainties.

A simple and direct yet powerful presentation of one of the foundational contradictions of human identity is the track titled "Hafta Have You." The text or lyrics of this track consist entirely of repetition by a male voice of the three words of the title. The phrase begins as a chant, reiterated again and again and again, beginning with a tone of determination, gradually becoming increasingly emphatic, increasingly vehement, the voice becoming increasingly hoarse, the phrase repeated louder, faster, the speaker growing frantic, frenzied, maniacal, until at last literally choking on his own words, all speech ends. It is a bravura performance in the course of which we witness with our ears the way in which self-assertion, self-will and a relentless grasping after self-gratification result in self-destruction as the speaker disintegrates, wholly consumed by his own obsessive desire.

Among Nordine's most poetically potent, yet elusive, compositions is the track titled "7 +1," consisting of eight separate but inter-related spoken pieces, including an initial third person narrative followed by seven monologues. Nordine's comments on the liner notes describe "7 + 1" as comprising "eight statements of Christ identification, a psychiatric theology." Serving as a sort of preface to the sequence, a voice pronounces that "Some are dreamers and some are realists." This latter statement seems to provide a perspective on the consciousnesses the listener encounters in the separate pieces that follow. The question that would appear to be implicit in this comment is which of the figures presented in "7 +1" are dreamers and which are realists: are those realists who attempt to derive gain from the material world, seeking power or pleasure, or if the world of the spirit is primary, then are those who think of themselves as realists the real dreamers? In a similar fashion, those who appear to be dreamers (naïve idealists) are only such if the physical realm of existence is the primary and exclusive reality; if that is not the case, then those who cultivate spiritual values are the true realists.

The first piece is titled "Kid in galoshes, walking across puddle." The vignette is narrated in the third person by one who has access to the thoughts and emotions of a young boy who overcomes his fear of stepping into and crossing to the far side of a large rain puddle, an expanse of water which seems to him as broad and as deep as a lake or a sea. The event is depicted as being momentous, dividing past from future, and as "the beginning of miracles," the boy "stamping with miracles" as he crosses the water. The child's triumph over his fear in walking over the puddle may be seen as a parallel to the incident in the New Testament where Christ and Peter walk upon the Sea of Galilee – a victory of the spirit over the limitations of the physical, material world. The boy's lonely act of courage takes place under and against the "thundering eye" of the Mother (apparently Nature.) The vignette concludes with the narrator observing that "everyone is afraid of the deep," and urging us all to "splash against the emptying eye," an exhortation, I take it, to strive and strain against limitations of fear and resignation.

Confinement is the theme of the next piece in the sequence, "All boxed in." The narrator of this monologue is imprisoned within his own consciousness, constricted within imaginary walls, seeking escape. The only freedom he achieves is that of appreciating the humor of his position and of accepting his madness. This may be seen to represent a kind of qualified redemption, or at least an initial step toward redemption. The piece seems to suggest that our personal, private incarcerations – psychological or spiritual – are of our own making and that our liberation from these self-constructed dungeons is also a matter that can only be pursued in the solitude of our minds and souls. "We think of the key, each in his prison," T.S. Eliot writes in *The Waste Land,* "thinking of the key, each confirms a prison." [25]

An insight – incipient, incomplete – similar to that of the prisoner in the foregoing piece seems also to have been achieved by the narrator of the "Idiot Saint's Self-Portrait." The contrasts that structure the piece are those of time-past and time-present ("somethen" versus "somenow.") In the past, the narrator relished the notion of his own martyrdom, foreseeing his death at the hands of a shouting crowd who despised him. Then, abruptly, he experienced an unexpected apprehension of his own condition in the world: "Instead, I saw myself, the somenow of me." This cryptic epiphany seems to suggest a sudden mind-toppling sense of the sheer strangeness of self-conscious selfhood, the mystery of being. Such an insight could mark the beginning of a deeper discernment concerning the nature of existence and the nature of the self.

The situation of the speaker of "Trying to Get the Point," the next monologue in the sequence, is unclear. Are the words spoken by a schizophrenic who hears imaginary voices or by an aspiring mystic who possesses a tenuous contact with the realm of spirits? The speaker strains to make sense of what he is hearing, draws inferences, but then dismisses his conclusions, only to reconsider them again. In common with other narrators of "7 + 1," the anonymous speaker here is isolated, alienated, endeavouring to discover some kind of coherence and personal purpose in the inexplicable world he inhabits. In a sense, the speaker's attempts to find order and meaning among the confusing voices, "the fugue of conversation" to which he listens and which he only partially comprehends, may be seen as analogous to the human situation, to the enduring human quest for meaning. Like him, we would all wish to "pick up the pieces of say and puzzle them together;" like him, we would all wish to make sense of and respond appropriately to the mystery in which we find ourselves.

A more expansive, more complex epiphany is delineated by the speaker of "Truth," the next piece in the "7 +1" sequence. The speaker recounts the stages of his struggle to understand the nature of truth and his relationship to others, beginning with a realization that "the huge and indifferent truth" is to be found everywhere, truth upon truth, and truth within truth. This perception of the vastness and varieties, the intricacies and subtleties of the truth leads him to understand the essential likeness that obtains among our individual minds and how our separate selves are inter-related. Despite having experienced this insight, the speaker's new understanding of his own self in relation to other selves remains limited by a residual egotistical desire to impose his identity and ideas upon others: "I wanted you to be me." Unable to quell this blind infantile impulse, the speaker retreats for a time into suspicion and animus, into guile and cunning in his relations with others, and into self-inflicted torments in his relation to himself. These events are, however, in the past, and his monologue concludes in the present, where he has undergone a revelation that it is by the power of love only that separations between humans can be bridged. With the apprehension of this high truth, the speaker declares, all is forever altered: "everything can never be the same again." This awareness of the sovereign and mysterious power of love is, indeed, a true expression of "Christ identification," to quote again the liner notes to "7 +1." In this monologue, the image of a further "shore" and "walking across" boundaries, together with the concluding triumphant tone, resonate with similar imagery and a similar tone in "Kid in Galoshes," the first piece in the "7 +1" sequence. The implication is, perhaps, that love is not less a miracle than walking on water.

In contrast to "Truth," the next track in the sequence, titled "Me, the Sly Fox, not so Sly," is an internal monologue delivered by a gloating, boastful, richly self-satisfied, yet ultimately self-deceiving speaker. The speaker celebrates his own "deviousness" and "cunning," takes pleasure in seeing himself as "crafty," and exults in the titles he bestows upon himself of "general" and "master." Yet, all his vaunted power is illusory, his exalted achievements imaginary. His insatiably famished ego has collapsed into a black hole of solipsism. For all his studied aloofness and smug self-approbation, the speaker's psychological situation is much like that of the narrator of "All Boxed In," close confinement within the prison of the isolated self, a condition diametric to that of "Christ-imitation." The qualifying clause – "not so sly" – of the title of the piece suggests the presence of a persistent and potentially devastating doubt. Again, we are presented with the implicit question: in the last analysis, who among us are the dreamers and who the realists?

The penultimate piece in the "7 + 1" sequence is "Spring Rain." This is a monologue spoken or thought by the falling spring rain and addressed directly and explicitly to the world below, including humankind. The rain is aware that it will perish upon contact with the earth but that its demise will be the necessary catalyst for the spring resurrection of vegetation. The raindrops will sink into the earth, entering "the kingdom of worms," (both literally, i.e. the subsoil and substratum, and figuratively, i.e. death) but through death will be transformed into new life. The iridescent rain drops, painting their descent with the colors of the spectrum as they fall, will become in the dark earth the blending and sum of all colors, that is, white. ("I am going to white.") The sacrifice of the falling spring rain, joyously embracing its necessary death, ("Come, sweet death") unafraid to lose its identity in transformation and renewal, in fullness and fertility, may be seen to be a parallel to the death and resurrection of Christ. I think this is suggested in the line: "Take me, my descent is your resurrection." Such selflessness, such benevolence and self-giving in love stands in clear contrast to the self-absorption and self-seeking of isolate egos that has been dramatized in other sections of the "7 + 1" sequence.

By its antecedent likeness, the "Spring Rain" segment prefigures the final component of the sequence, a piece titled "7 + 1 No Locks." Again, this is a monologue spoken to specific listeners –

addressed as "you" – and, as the title suggests, the theme is that of openness and invitation, of freedom from guile or wariness, of being freely available and accessible. The speaker is unidentified but the imagery, tone and tenor of the monologue clearly suggests that this is the risen Christ. The speaker announces at the outset that "I have come winking back," and alludes to wounds on his hands, wounds which he likens to "eyes," or vehicles of vision. He invites his listeners to touch his wounds, "then see me." His resurrection causes Christ to smile and laugh, to manifest playfulness and joy, and to proclaim a new "game" in which the rule is "we will all be winners." He also declares that – through his death and resurrection – "I have become fulcrum. I can explain yourself. What can you do but give me you?" Moreover, "you have become me, us is one." The joyousness, the celebration of unity and renewal, the sense of victory and proclamation of a new vision all stand apart from and run counter to the psychic darkness and fragmentation, the alienation and confusion of many of the previous speakers in the sequence. I believe that is why the collective title of the sequence is "7 + 1," in that the first seven pieces constitute a disparate group of voices representing various levels of spiritual awareness or its absence, whereas the final piece is uniquely numinous, drawing together and resolving the themes and motifs of the previous segments. What was *locked,* restrained, restricted, and seeking release in the early sections of the sequence, (the spirit imprisoned by the ego) has in the final segment been *unlocked,* set at liberty, a liberty that is universally accessible. The far shore of the perilous deep-fathomed sea – as imaged in "Kid in Galoshes" – has been triumphantly attained, and can be reached by all.

Hideous, horrific, hallucinated, gaudy and grim, "The Climber," the final cut on *Next,* holds a mirror to the obsessions and excesses, the faults and failings of our age.

This nightmarish track is narrated by a third-person speaker who describes a film being projected on a cinema screen and the reaction of the theatre audience viewing the film. The action depicted in the movie centers upon a midget, named Otto, ascending a living tower of glamorous women each sitting on the other's shoulders. At the pinnacle of the tower sits an 87 year old unmarried woman in a ragged wedding dress. When, at length, Otto attains the top of the tower, he claims his hideous, withered bride and is, in turn, claimed by her, as she drags him away with an umbilical cord wound around his neck.

Otto, a mix of races and religions, may be seen as a metaphoric embodiment of humanity at large, a representative everyman. "He plays for us," we are told. His stunted stature suggests, I believe, a spiritual runtishness or arrested development general to our age. He is described by the narrator as being "boasting, cunning, determined, egotistical, fanatic, grotesque, haughty," characteristics common, of course, to most human beings. Otto's attraction to a woman of such advanced age (in preference to the nubile beauties he bypasses during his climb) would seem to indicate some kind of Oedipal fixation (reinforced by the image of the umbilical cord) which can be seen as an indication of psychic development arrested at an infantile stage. His being "dragged away" by means of an umbilical cord wound round his neck would seem to suggest a loss of individual autonomy and a regression to an infantile state. In brief, Otto's successful attainment of the top of the tower is, in no sense, a triumph, unless it is viewed as a victory for the fulfilment of a regressive and retrograde obsession.

The movie, the narrator informs us, is filmed in black-and-white and "narrow vision." However, after the climax of the plot action, the film suddenly changes to "full-color, full screen, full everything" as a giant megaphone intrudes upon the scene, ominously pronouncing *mene mene tekel upharsin.* These words, it will be remembered, are the famous "handwriting on the wall," occurring during Belshazzar's debauched feast. The words are a divine warning to Belshazzar and his lords, interpreted as meaning "you have been weighed on the scales and found wanting," and "your days are numbered." [26] The "narrow vision" of the contem-porary hedonistic, materialist world – the world that worships pleasure and possessions – has thus been reproved and forewarned.

As if in immediate fulfilment of the divine prophecy, order both in the film and in the theatre begins instantly to disintegrate: on screen the human tower of attractive women collapses, the audience breaks into wild uproar, and the theatre is invaded by a thousand midgets demanding their compensatory reward. A futile (if robust: "leaded popcorn") attempt is made by the forces of order (the Marine Corps) to quell the upheaval. Disaster is avoided only when distraction is provided. Just as the audience is calling for the destruction of the screen, a Bugs Bunny cartoon is shown, immediately pacifying all insurgent impulses among the moviegoers.

"The Climber" is a critique of several inter-related aspects of the modern world. These include – in addition to a biting commentary on bland materialism and blind hedonism – the psychological addiction of mass audiences to diversion, and the mindless, meaningless pap that is provided to them by the media industries. The shallow, trivial entertainment that is offered to and consumed by audiences is seen to represent a modern day parallel to Belshazzar's feast at which holy vessels taken from the temple were desecrated by their profane use in feasting and drinking wine. In "The Climber" the female body and the sexual impulse are similarly desecrated by their exploitation as vehicles of voyeuristic titillation. Women on screen are reduced to dehumanized anonymity with names such as "You Name Her," "Supercilious Smile," "Who Cares," and "Miss Teeth." The words of celebrated authors such as Ariosto, Bacon, Goethe, Camus, Faulkner, Hemingway and the Hebrew prophet Ezra are misappropriated as lines of dialogue in the inane, inconsequential film being shown in the theatre. This, too, is irreverence, a defilement of that which should be honored. Like Balshazzar and his lords, the film writers, the film director, and all those involved in the production and distribution of such a film, together with the audience that desires and devours it, have all reverted to idolatry, an idolatry of cheap stimulation, wretched excess and empty spectacle.

The audience requires entertainment to quell what would seem to be a secret, barely suppressed desperation, a void within, perhaps a latent awareness of their inauthentic lives as passive consumers of vulgar, meaningless distraction. The forces of order (represented here by the Marines in the aisles and whoever is in the projection booth) likewise need entertainment as a means to soothe and divert the masses who without ever novel and extravagant forms of amusement quickly become agitated and aggressive. In its efforts to provide suitably sensational and vacuous diversions, the entertainment industry degrades and debases everything it touches from human beauty to the human "search for love and meaning," travestied in Otto's ascent of the tower of female flesh. With the timely intervention of a Bugs Bunny cartoon even the awful wonder of a divine warning can quickly be effaced from memory.

Ranging from chants to rants, from poetic monologues to prose vignettes, from free verse to metered, end-rhymed verse, from the wryly comic to the deeply unsettling, from the maniacal to the reverent, *Next* confirms the variety and originality of Nordine's recorded spoken word performances and makes clearer the essential unity of his vision, a worldview which deplores all instances of egotism and selfishness, narrow materialism and mindless hedonism, and celebrates an expansive, receptive stance, wonder, humor, and an ethos that chafes at conventions and limitations. On the evidence of these first three LPs, all made during the 1950s, we see clearly the affinities between Nordine's work and the cultural radicalism and hip sensibility as manifest during that era: satirical treatment of social and psychological issues, an idiosyncratic perspective on the human situation and a sense that the solution to its myriad ills is ultimately spiritual in nature, jabs and jolts against conformity, complacency and consumerism, jazz as creative model and inspiration, a freewheeling spirit of artistic experimentation and a reaching out for new modes of expression.

A further portion of Nordine's trenchant whimsy and quirky subversion is to be found on *Word Jazz Volume II*. [27] Among the album's most acute tracks is "Confessions of 349-18-5171," an unheroic fable of failure and success in the social, economic and personal realms of American life. A first person narrator recounts the story of his life, growing up in a small Midwestern town as the son of a popular local clergyman. During his early life there all seems wholesome and idyllic, but this stability is thrown into disorder by the arrival of an itinerant "pitchman," an aggressive, high-pressure, self-promoting, self-styled debater who – as a form of public entertainment – offers to argue against the existence of God. Reluctantly accepting the pitchman's challenge, the narrator's father is decisively defeated in debate by his atheist opponent, a man of "shallow understanding" but "sparkling wit." Humiliated and devastated, the narrator's father leaves town and the now orphaned narrator becomes an object of contempt and persecution by his fellow townsmen. Unable to earn a living, the narrator, too, leaves town and pursues a life elsewhere, working at a number of unskilled jobs.

His first job is as an encyclopedia salesman, a task he vigorously undertakes in the proud belief that he is conveying to his customers "all the world's knowledge." Few, however, are interested in acquiring such a magnificent treasure as that and so the narrator descends the ladder of employment to its lowest rung and from there proceeds downward to unemployment and penury. Having reached this nadir, however, his fortunes begin to turn. Upon witnessing two bullies tormenting a waitress, he immediately joins them in their villainy, so impressing them by this act of sordid solidarity that they invite him to go bowling with them. In consequence, he experiences an epiphany, a "great secret" is revealed to him: "Everyone loves themselves more than they love anyone else." This marks the beginning of his rehabilitation in the world. He now begins to align himself with popular taste and behavior. He buys the same type of necktie as everyone else is wearing and his taste in neckties is admired. He determines to be like everyone else in all respects, conscientiously meeting the expectations and conforming to the standards of others and soon has a lucrative and respected position as a commercial radio announcer (in which, as he says, he takes "understandable pride") pitching to the public products such as deodorant.

As the title of the track suggests, issues of identity and individuality are central here. In the narrator's tale, we perceive how tentative and tenuous a thing personal identity is and how much it may derive from the approval of a community, the acceptance of others. We see, too, how easily and willingly personal integrity can be relinquished in order to achieve social status. And we are confronted with an unpleasant reminder that at the center of each outwardly affable social identity lies a hard, dark core of self-serving, self-savouring egotism.

"Confessions of 349-18-5171" may also be seen as a commentary on the archetypal American success story, a critique of the American myth of success. Typically, in works such as *The Autobiography of Benjamin Franklin* or in the novels of Horatio Alger, upward economic progress, from modest beginnings to "the pinnacle," is achieved through honesty, hard work and perseverance; virtue and a strict work ethic are rewarded. [28] In contrast, in Nordine's "Confessions," the protagonist succeeds through cruelty, deception and conformity. He not only compromises his integrity, he surrenders it altogether. In so doing, he becomes – not the upright son of his earnest clergyman father – but the illegitimate son of the satanic pitchman who cynically gains his livelihood by shallow cleverness. For in the end, the narrator has himself become a pitchman, pitching to his vulnerable, gullible listening audience fear of social rejection due to body odor and salvation-through-deodorant.

The view of human character suggested in "Confessions" is anything but favorable. The incidents recounted by the narrator furnish proof of human fickleness and perfidy, cruelty and deceit. While "all the world's knowledge" in convenient encyclopaedic form excites no interest and finds no buyers, anti-perspirants are accepted as indispensable to modern man. We are seen to inhabit a world in which "shallow understanding and sparkling wit" so often trump serious-minded and heartfelt beliefs and where self-infatuation is too often the bedrock beneath a seemingly benign social mask. Yet in characteristic Nordine fashion, this dark tale is told with dexterous touches of dry humor, as when, for example, we are told that out of "civic pride" the narrator's idyllic hometown of Cherokee, Iowa deceptively inflates its population by including in its census count the inmates of the nearby State Insane Asylum, or how on the occasion of the great debate in the town gymnasium between the atheist pitchman and the narrator's clergyman father, the local eight piece American Legion band plays a Sousa march "almost in tune." Another darkly humorous incident is when – contrary to every civilized tradition, every heroic code and every romantic formula – the narrator, rather than defending and rescuing the waitress who is being mistreated by two bullies, instead, assists her assailants. And, as a final touch, there is the irony of the sense of "understandable pride" felt by the narrator (who, it will be remembered, originally aspired to a career as a clergyman) in his current status as a commercial announcer, a servant of Mammon, celebrating a trivial product in a silly manner.

Another fable illustrating the adverse consequences of giving unrestricted liberty to the drives and desires of the ego is "Reaching into In." In this tale, a man becomes obsessed with the notion of reaching the utter innermost constituent of his being. This quixotic, all-consuming goal causes him to neglect vital human relations. His self-absorption alienates his wife, his children and his friends. Inwardly, he obstinately opposes the three virtues of Faith, Hope and Charity, thus contending against what is best in himself. And, in the end, having in this manner laid waste both to his outer and his inner life, his perverse endeavor proves to be futile. He has forfeited everything of value and has gained nothing. Surrendering to the centripetal pull of self-reflexivity is seen ultimately to end in a kind of psychic autocannibalism.

Even the milder and more common forms of self-interest may have unintended consequences, as seen in "Original Sin." Here, a chain of cause-and-effect unfolds: a carefully lived, "regular, regulated life" is suddenly disturbed by the presence of rats in the cellar of a house, this discovery induces inordinate fear in the mind of the protagonist, who then slays the invading rodents by means of rat poison. Fearful now of the presence in his house of the unused portion of the rat poison, the protagonist undertakes to rid himself of it by throwing it out of his car window while driving to work, after which, we are told by the narrator, the man never again gave the matter a second thought. His action in jettisoning the poison, though not malicious in intent, has dire consequences for others (whose lives he never considered). A blameless dog, "a poet dog," unknowingly consumes the poison and dies. That, to be sure, would be sin enough, but worse than that, "every neighbor in that neighborhood has a theory as to which lousy neighbour poisoned the dog." A single, careless, thoughtless act of self-preservation on the part of the protagonist sows death and discord among the innocent. It is a cautionary tale: the poison of casual egoism can sometimes serve to poison the human community.

In one sense, "Spectrum," (recalling "The Sound Museum") could be seen as an exercise in synaesthesia, a counterpart to Arthur Rimbaud's celebrated "Sonnet des Voyelles," in which the poet assigns colors to each vowel. [29] In order to "listen to colors," the narrator of this track tells us, "an open eye" is required. But, deeper than this level of meaning, in the narrator's characterization of the individual colors there would seem to be an implication of something sombre and unsettling. Each of the seven colors mentioned in the track is seen to correspond with one of the Seven Deadly Sins: "red, wearing pride," "covetous orange," "lustful yellow," "angry green," "glutinous blue," "envious indigo," and "slothful violet." In ascribing to colors certain inherent negative qualities, there seems to be a suggestion here of a fallenness (or disposition toward sin or evil) at the core of the phenomenal world. Even at the heart of color there is seen to be a hidden, essential darkness.

Living our lives in a fallen world, it follows that language and human relations also become debased, as expressed in the dramatic monologue titled "So and So." Let me pause here, to make clear that the concept of a fallen world is not peculiar to Jewish and Christian doctrine but seems to be universal. The mythographer Mircea Eliade names this notion "the paradise myth," according to which our primordial human situation was one of harmony with Heaven. Eliade explains that – across cultures – common to the paradise myth is the premise that primordial humanity enjoyed "a beatitude, a spontaneity and freedom ... lost in consequence of the *fall* – that is, of what followed upon the mythical event that caused the *rupture* between Heaven and Earth." [30] Such a rupture is apparent in "So and So" which takes as its subject disparaging and malicious talk and its consequences (including loss of employment). The most striking feature of the monologue is, however, the regular and repeated substitution by the speaker of the phrase "so and so" for the particular names of persons and things in the incident he is relating. The speaker's rampant overuse of this lazy and imprecise phrase sows a confusion in the mind of the listener that mirrors the conflicts among the principals involved in the speaker's tale. Not only are social relations here shown to be disharmonious but the abuse of language is shown to contribute signally to the general human muddle. Significantly, the phrase "so and so" is itself ambiguous, meaning both an unnamed or unspecified person or thing and an offensive or disagreeable person.

Whatever may be the misuse and corruption of language in the world, music in *Word Jazz*

Volume II is celebrated as a sovereign and salutary art form with its own grammar and vocabulary. In the track titled "There's a She and a He," a love story is chanted in sing-song rhythm, with musical passages replacing key words in the narrative. The substitution of mere abstract tonal patterns for words at intervals on the track affirms the peculiar expressive power of music, with its capacity to convey meanings and communicate states of mind, to arouse emotions and evoke moods. Further to this argument, "Adult Kindergarten" is another upbeat homage to the mysterious potency of music, in this instance its power to loosen social inhibitions and summon joy and a sense of community among those who collaborate to create it. The track presents a disparate group of people meeting weekly to play jazz, using for their instruments common household objects such as a carpet, Venetian blinds, a table, a waste basket and a child's toy piano. "Adult Kindergarten" suggests that the ordinary and commonplace can become vehicles of pleasure and satisfaction, that the bounds of our ordinary personalities can be exceeded, and we can thus attain a richer, fuller state of being, regaining something of the innocence and unselfconscious creative elation of children. In contrast to the greed and self-seeking depicted on other cuts on *Word Jazz Volume II* (and elsewhere among Nordine's work), the amateur musicians who make up the "Adult Kindergarten" are pursuing neither status nor power, nor material or monetary gain, nor some other utilitarian goal, but are, instead, absorbed in a collective, creative endeavour, one that might be said (citing the justly famous phrase of *The Declaration of Independence*) to constitute a commendable illustration of "the pursuit of happiness."

The qualities of wonder and curiosity are endorsed in "Fireflies," while "You're Getting Better" may be seen as a form of self-improving autosuggestion in the manner of Émile Coué (1857 – 1926), whose famous therapeutic mantra was "Everyday, in every way, I'm getting better and better." Nordine transforms this incantation into a kind of self-help session for beleagured non-conformists, encouraging them to maintain their resistance to the manifold social and commercial pressures brought to bear upon them. In soothing, approving tones the speaker attempts to hearten his farflung dissident listeners, affirming that they are making progress in their praiseworthy practice of questioning accepted values and attitudes, divesting themselves of superfluous material possessions, and striving to live a life that is "more naked, more free." If they persist, they will prevail, he promises. In the meantime, "make it on your own." In the face of sameness, blandness and orthodoxy, Nordine once again gives nourishment to hip individualism.

The track titled "Lesson No. 1" on *Word Jazz Volume II* eludes my understanding even as it piques my curiosity. It seems to be a kind of parable or a Zen-like *koan*. The piece enumerates and very briefly describes a series of eight lessons, the aim or end of which is unspecified. Lesson No. 1, we are told, "is mysteriously simple." Thereafter, the narrator informs us, the lessons become increasing complicated and self-referential, each new lesson seemingly consisting of a new level of awareness concerning the previous lesson, reacting to it with fear, doubt or disapproval. After a series of complexities and contradictions, the final lesson, lesson no. 8, is described as being "mysteriously simple." I think the operative word here is the adverb: "mysteriously." The first and last lessons are not "deceptively simple," but "mysteriously simple," a phrase which is oxymoronic, a paradox. I am reminded of the Zen proverb: "Before I sought enlightenment, the mountains were mountains and the rivers were rivers. While I sought enlightenment, the mountains were not mountains and the rivers were not rivers. After I attained enlightenment, the mountains were mountains and the rivers were rivers." [31] I am also reminded of a phrase from T.S. Eliot's "Little Gidding," in which the poet speaks of arriving finally at "A condition of complete simplicity (costing not less than everything.)" [32]

In alluding to the two quotations cited above, I am attempting to approach what is for me the felt meaning of "Lesson No. 1." The circular progression of the sequence of lessons does not suggest to me a futile or fruitless cycle, a vain return, as it were, to square one, but rather a gradual advance, a development that, in the end, revisits and more deeply comprehends the nature of the point of origin and departure. By this, I mean to say the person who has experienced the first seven lessons, regains with the eighth lesson the lost knowledge of things being "mysteriously simple." My sense of the series of lessons is one of a progress, an unfolding of the mind, a deepening awareness that leads finally to a new clarity, to a state of simplicity not as a given (as in the first of the lessons) but as something earned, achieved, a new, higher, stronger, truer simplicity tempered by the intervening loss of original simplicity. Simplicity, it would seem, is no simple matter, but endlessly mysterious.

Endlessly mysterious, too, endlessly fascinating and baffling, sad and laughable is, for Nordine, the state of things – the behaviors, claims and notions, the patterns and manifestations that distinguish the particular spacetime coordinates we inhabit, our erratic era, our frivolous, frightened lives. These topics are treated once again in the tracks gathered on *Stare with your Ears*. [33] In contrast to earlier word jazz LPs, featuring prose fables, prose poems, vignettes, playlets and dramatic monologues, *Stare with your Ears* consists exclusively of song lyrics and poems, metrically regular and end-rhymed. There are ballads, blues, waltzes and rhythmic recitations, all with musical accompaniment. Also in contrast to earlier word jazz LPs which made use of (ever fewer) sound effects, the audio recording techniques employed in creating this collection are confined to electronic voice distortion and the overdubbing of Nordine's voice to create the effect of an echo of or response to the primary narrative voice. A final distinction between *Stare with your Ears* and previous albums by Nordine is that of mood; the thirteen tracks collected here seem (with two exceptions) time-haunted, death-haunted, permeated with a sense of peril, loss and melancholy.

The first track on *Stare with your Ears* may be seen as a kind of thematic prologue to or premise of the tracks that follow. Titled "Island," and subtitled "John's Island Redonne," the text is an ironic riposte to an often cited passage from John Donne's "Devotions Upon Emergent Occasions: Meditation XVII." [34] The narrator of "Island" reverses Donne's argument that individuals are interconnected in a larger human and ultimately divine unity and, instead, asserts his independence and self-sufficiency in what he sees as a sea of life strewn with other isolate ego-islands. Significantly, the word "me" is recurrent in this short piece. The first lines of the track are: "I got me this island / that I'm calling me." This colloquial construction ("I got me") is called a personal dative and is seen by linguists as implying that the event that the verb describes matters to or satisfies the subject in some sense. [35] From the first statement, then, the self-complacency of the narrator is patent. This motif is developed and in the final lines the narrator expresses a sense of the fruitlessness of aspiring to personal development or self-transformation. Our identities, he pronounces, are a given, immutable; we cannot alter them, we can only accept them: "the island you get / is the island you got."

The destructive consequences of this self-enclosed, psychologically static condition – the attachments, attitudes and behaviours that proceed from it – are instanced in a number of other tracks on the LP. "Angel's Lament," for example, is a story-in-song concerning a squandered inheritance. The young heirs to an industrious, thrifty old couple, having just received their share of their parents' bequest, travel to Las Vegas in the hope of doubling their money. Instead, in a short spell of unrestrained and luckless gambling at dice and cards, the heirs lose all that they have received.

Lured by what the historian Jim Cullen calls Las Vegas' "promise of secular fulfilment," their naïve greed is their undoing. [36] The contrast between the ethos of hard work, frugality and self-sacrifice as practiced by the parents and the self-indulgent impetuousness and imprudence of the children suggests two fundamentally different orientations toward existence: one of humility and modesty, the other of egotistic entitlement. The song's refrain – " who cares about winter / the first day of spring" – points to a parallel form of disregard for consequences, a wilful ignorance leading inevitably to a kind of spiritual impoverishment. The song is narrated by an angel, implying an extramundane perspective on human folly. Time runs on, the angel reminds us, until it runs out, and when it does then all that matters in ones life is – not money or material possessions – but only having felt and expressed love.

Time is again a central motif in "Ballad of the Final Page." The song describes a bar called The Final Page, frequented by the aged and the unrepentant. The customers here – obstinately flawed – are living out their last weeks and months, departing one by one for the next world. Until the very end, though, they persist in their misdeeds: anger, indifference to others, drunkenness, gluttony, lust and greed. There is in the song a pervading sense of lives wasted, of individuals trapped in the squalid roles they have chosen or been assigned, of minds close-confined by compulsions and automatic patterns of behaviour.

An equally dark, more comprehensive portrayal of the human situation is expressed in "Seven Ways of the Meek." Deploying puns, literary and Biblical allusions, (most frequently to The Sermon on the Mount) the eight verses of this lyric depict a world awry, a world in which everyone and everything is tainted and sundered and all endeavors futile, a world whose inhabitants – like rodents on a treadmill – trudge bleakly through the days of the week: Dumbday, Bluesday, Endsday, Blursday, Cryday, Shatterday and Stunday. Already at the outset of the first day, we are told, things begin to fail and fall apart, and as the weekdays succeed each other, the woes and misfortunes multiply. "Evil," the narrator informs us, "has sufficiencies equal to the day," and the seven-day week consists of "seven kinds of cruel." There is, in the end, no conclusion, no resolution, no hope of release or rescue, for we know that the cycle of weekdays will begin again, over and over, even as individual lives expire. In the interim, other than cynicism and sensualism, anxiety and alcoholic oblivion, there seems to be no response to their plight on the part of the citizens of this waste land, whose names suggest the narrow limitations of their awareness: Mister Maybe, Lady Snake, Edgy,

Whimper, Doctor No No, Mister Smithereens, Doubtful Tommy and others. Among them, none are meek, all are lost and doomed.

A further allegory of the human condition, presenting a deeper vision of the fallen world, is furnished in "Once upon a You Know What." The events described in the lyric have occurred in a distant past, yet their effects are seen to continue to reverberate in the present. The temporal setting, we are told, is "old as now," an eternal trans-temporal moment, simultaneously past and present, ancient and current. In a mysterious, mythical past, foundational to historical time, humankind sought an explanation for existence: the why and how of living. Replying to their query, an entity named Mr. Hoodwink deceived these earnest questioners, convincing them that the only goal and purpose in life is material wealth. In consequence, values such as compassion became dormant, pangs of conscience were assuaged by hedonistic distraction, and the sense of awe and wonder was lost, later to expire. In opposition to this sorry state of things stand two occurrences, one in the past, the other still to happen. The first of these is the resurrection, the other is the second coming. When the "lamb" returns, the "simple truth" will be established, finally and definitively abolishing the original deception perpetrated by

Mr. Hoodwink which made of the world a bewildering "puzzle park."

Employing personified allegorical characters, such as Wonder Why, Mr. Hoodwink, Gives-a-Damn, Guilty and Gee Whiz, "Once upon a You Know What" is essentially a nursery rhyme, fairytale-like retelling of the fall and redemption of humankind. In seven quatrains, we are presented with a potent vision of the human spiritual condition encompassing the past, present and future. The final line of the lyric is startling and enigmatic: "God is such a slave." I believe this pronouncement is a reference to St. Paul's description of Christ who "put aside his divinity and became a slave out of love for us." [37] God may be seen to have become a slave by entering into and sharing human pain and desolation, undertaking selfless service to humankind, remaining obedient even in the face of torture and death that the scripture might be fulfilled.

It will not have escaped the notice of attentive word jazz fans, nor of readers of this monograph, that in Nordine's work the state of the world, with its corruption, its violence, its hectic pursuit of wealth, pleasure, power and status is often contrasted to spiritual values and attitudes, imaged in terms of Christian spirituality. Allusions to and parallels with Christian scriptures are central to several key word jazz tracks, including "

Junkman" and "7 + 1," but such themes and devices are proffered to the listener in an oblique and non-doctrinaire manner, comparable in a sense to the deep but often subtle roots of jazz music in spirituals and gospel hymns.

In each its way, "Mister Blister" and "Smelts" add evidence to an implicit argument that creation itself is at its heart remorseless and malevolent. The former track, despite its apparent light touch, treats a minor but not insignificant example of "honest to goodness evil," that is the vulnerability of our frail, fragile human flesh to injury and infection. The narrator characterizes the perpetrators "Mister Blister" and his sister "Fester" as cunning, deceitful and malicious, while the refrain ("as the world goes around and around and around ...") suggests that these are the conditions under which we must live and we can only resign ourselves to the innate hostility of the physical world. A similar dark vision informs "Smelts," in which these small fish, driven by spawning instinct, are portrayed as doomed to be netted and eaten by humans. Seeking to perpetuate life, these pitiful creatures encounter death. Perhaps this short lyric is a reminder that ultimately we are all pitiful creatures driven by reproductive instincts and that a "net" may be said to be lie in wait for us, too.

The theme of mortality is further considered – at a more personal level – in "Fadeaway Stranger" and "Scratch," both narrated in the first person. The former concerns the acute sense of separation from his deceased father that haunts the narrator of the track, the implacable knowledge that in the infinitely distant, unreachable place where his father has gone "sunset is light years / ahead of the dawn." In "Scratch," the narrator addresses his dog, acknowledging their common transience and ignorance in the face of the mystery of existence. Although the present moment seems secure and enduring, the narrator muses, it is, in reality, perilous and precarious, ever situated "right next to where endings begin." This sad awareness causes him to long for a realm of being where there is final safety, a place "where laughter / is louder than grief." But the closing lines of the lyric, echoing the opening lines, suggest a stoic resumption of mundane duties on the part of the narrator and a kind of rueful resignation to the world as it is.

Deeper, though, than our conscious adjustments to and accommodations with the world lie bleak inner landscapes of loss, disorientation, fear, sorrow and estrangement. These dark substrata accumulate pressure and stress and thrust upward, causing fissures and fractures in our surface consciousness, emitting their energy into our minds in the form of depression, despondency, "the blues."

This condition is expressed in two tracks: "Cracks in the Ceiling" and "Inchoate Blues." The narrator of first of these wakes in his bed, opening his eyes to study the cracked ceiling above him, its topography suggesting to him a terrain of pain, inhabited by cries and sly shadows, malicious jokers, deceitful laughers, a blind referee, a drunk, a trickster, and an angel whose name is "ain't." In the country he sees spread out across the ceiling above him there is only failure, absence, sordidness, disintegration, confusion, crime and venality. It is a realm where souls yearn for something else, something other, but are likened, in the end, to "frozen fireflies," their aspirations nullified. In a like manner, "Inchoate Blues" depicts a dejected mood of mind, characterized by "inner distortions / magnified fears," distress, dysphoria and a pervasive sense of futility. Aware that even his attempts to communicate his pain and plight are merely repetitions of what others similarly afflicted have already expressed, unable even to weep, he sees himself as "a seeker / partially blind," caught in unending, irresolvable "inchoate blues."

Counterpointing the rather sombre tenor of the greater number of tracks on *Stare with your Ears* are two pieces celebrating poetic possibilities latent in the conventional and commonplace. "Alphabet" reconceives the letters of the Roman alphabet, perceiving each as a picture rather than as a symbol representing a speech sound. The letters are thus released from their fixed, practical functions and freed to return to their deepest origins as pictograms. Informing this playful exercise there is a sense that things need not be limited to their accepted roles, nor are they necessarily as immutable as they would appear to be. Surprises, discoveries are possible, requiring only that we set aside expectations and preconceptions and exercise a form of creative perception. In a similar manner, "Don't You Wish" overturns fixities of personal identity, encouraging us to expand our narrow conceptions of ourselves beyond predetermined categories and patterns, extending our conscious awareness to encompass a myriad of shapes, sounds and sensations, and in so doing experience the mystery and multiplicity of the wondrous world we habitually so routinely, so impercipiently inhabit. We need not, then, passively accept the world as given, we can, instead, in the manner of jazz musicians, conjure our own individual thought-jazz, improvise, as it were, upon the melodic lines and harmonic progression of our perceptions and our identities, and swing in each our own unique and inimitable way.

With *Triple Talk* (1984), Ken Nordine again deploys a full range of forms and techniques, including monologue, dialogue, interior dialogue, playlets, poems, music, sound effects, overdubbing and electronic voice distortion. [38] The tracks on *Triple Talk* can be seen to fall into two broad categories: the Weirdness Within and the Weirdness Without. These designations are, of course, rough and general and are not mutually exclusive; between the two classifications there are occasional connections and interactions. Tracks which I consider to belong to the first of these two categories are concerned with the inner world of the private mind, with issues of consciousness and identity, thought and memory, love and meaning, while those tracks which I regard as belonging to the second category deal with the external, social world of status and money, ambition and striving, conflict and isolation.

Before pondering those tracks I deem to be in the first category, it would be useful at this point to cite the incisive observations of Jeff Porter, author of *Lost Sound,* concerning a technique of which Nordine makes extensive use in *Triple Talk* and in many recordings made subsequently to the release of this album, that is the employment of a second voice (in addition to the narrator's voice) a distinctive, personal inner voice which replies and reacts to the narrator's voice. Porter identifies this second voice as that of "a bemused inner self ... presumably the narrator's alter ego or subconscious, who occasionally interjects with quips that ricochet off the narrative, sometimes in a parodic way. ... The other voice, that of the alter ego, is cheeky and digressive. It is a submerged voice that, compared to the full frequency range of the narrator's deep baritone, seems to come out of a small speaker. Nordine pioneered what musicians call today "the phone effect," filtering his alter ego's voice by reducing its high and low frequencies, with the result that it sounds as if it were spoken on a telephone. Essentially, the voice has been shrunk and loses authorial presence, which licences it to be parenthetical and even mischievous." [39]

The album opens with a track titled "Think a Thought," an interior dialogue of the kind described above, that is an aural representation of a narrator's private thoughts addressed to a deeper self, an entity to which (following Jeff Porter) I will hereinafter refer as the second voice or the alter ego. The topic being considered by the narrator is that of thought and memory. The narrator weighs the matter of the nature of thinking, wondering where thoughts originate and where they go. Whence, he asks, come the "notions, whims, intuitions, vagrancies" that seem suddenly to occupy our conscious awareness and then, after a time, dissipate? What ultimately becomes of our thoughts, do they return to the one Great Thought that is the universe? This speculation leads the narrator to consider the matter of memory, more specifically who is remembered after death and who is forgotten. He contrasts famous figures such as Christopher Columbus, remembered down through the centuries, with unremarkable lives, such as those of Sam Schwartz (local dry cleaner) and Frank Nichols (local bartender), both deceased and since forgotten. (The alter ego meanwhile proposes Matthew, Mark, Luke and John as imminent unforgotten figures.) Both narrator and alter ego agree on the false, empty nature of what the world celebrates as success, phrasing their convictions in opposite yet complementary constructions: "nothing fails like success," "nothing succeeds like failure." And both agree that worldly fame and fortune are fleeting and that human lives whether renowned or unremembered – like thoughts – disappear at last "into the immense design of things."

These musings take place against a manic, mechanical musical rhythm and a distant, high-pitched voice urgently enjoining both narrator and alter ego to "think a thought." In the course of the narrator's ruminations, this voice becomes increasingly frantic and more and more resembles the squawk of a parrot. These intrusive, unsettling sounds seem to suggest the frenzied, hectic, headlong character of our thoughts, the compulsions and fixations that assail our brains, leaving us but little space for quiet reflection and clarity. Of such a nature is the Weirdness Within.

The topic of memory is treated again in "Tape Recorder," where levels of consciousness within a man's mind converse and converge: a conscious, thinking mind imagining a tape recorder with total recall, "everything that ever happened to you or that happened to me," a voice from the narrator's childhood singing "Polly Wolly Doodle," and a third voice reciting Thomas Hood's poem "I remember, I remember." The voice of the conscious mind suddenly recognizes the voice from childhood and exclaims: "I was singing that silly song." A trivial memory, of course, but the connection suggests that the mind itself is a kind of tape recorder with total recall on which memories can be replayed, the present briefly suspended, time past reclaimed. The Thomas Hood poem supports the motif of vivid recollection of childhood by an adult mind, while contrasting the child's world of belief, joy and innocence to the adult burdens of doubt, guilt and sorrow. In both instances, the sudden sharp childhood memory of the narrator and Thomas Hood's recollections of his childhood, the experience of remembering serves to destabilize – however fleetingly – the subject's sense of time and space, implicitly calling identity itself into question as one sees oneself as another – as one was, that is, at the time of the remembered occurrence. In this manner, for a short duration, we dislocate ourselves, suspend ourselves. In the world within, it would seem, it's every mind against itself.

Since the first *Word Jazz* LP, the nature of time and its implications for our lives have engaged Nordine's imagination. Aspects of time are again considered on five tracks on *Triple Talk:* "Tape Recorder," (discussed above) "Noxt," "Tick Tock Fugue," "Infinite O'Clock" and "Ripples." In a whimsical fashion, "Noxt" ponders the question of the order in which things follow each other. What, the narrator wonders, occurs before that which happens next? How is the forthcoming event of the succeeding instant engendered, how is it determined? The narrator gives to this abstract concept of an immediately antecedent increment of time, the pre-incipient, still unmanifest origin of that which is next, the name of "noxt." He recognizes, though, that behind each such division of time, there are an "infinite number of noxts." (Penultimate, antepenultimate, preantepenulti-mate, pro-preantepenulimate, and so on, *ad infinitum* or perhaps back to the original cosmological singularity.) In a genial manner, the track induces a kind of ontological vertigo, confronting us with an infinite temporal regress, in which moment by mysterious moment we somehow strangely exist.

While time as imminent or impending was the subject of the narrator's speculations in "Noxt," the insomniac narrator of "Tick Tock Fugue" complains of "suffering from the Now," feeling himself trapped in time to the degree that he imagines himself uncomfortably confined within his alarm clock. In a sober, scientific fashion, the narrator ruminates upon the nature of time: "I thought time was continuous, that time is the movement of the first heavenly bodies. The things which sometimes are and sometimes are not are measured by time. Those things are said to be measured by time which have their beginning and their end in time, but the *now* of time is the same in all time, the measure of the first motion is the measure of all other motion. The before and after in the measure are derived from the change in the measured. The before and after are in time according as they are found in motion." As the narrator pursues this line of thought, a second voice pronounces that "now is the time," then slowly recites the old nursery rhyme foretelling children's fates according to the day of the week on which they were born: "Monday's child is fair of face ..." etc.

The two voices may be seen to represent two views of time. The voice of the narrator attempts to comprehend the progression of time according to the laws of physics, while puzzling over the disconcerting circumstance that "the now of time is the same in all time," and that we are forever caught in the now. In contrast to the vast temporal vistas contemplated by the narrator, the second voice proclaims a fixed view of time and human fate, time rigidly standardized as a cyclical seven day week, individual destinies determined in advance, all depending upon the day of their birth. The opposition of these two voices and views remains unresolved, interrupted by the ringing of an alarm clock, summoning the sleeper to the world of necessity and obligation where time is an instrument of social organization. This transition is heralded by a shrill, strident voice commanding: "get up, you've got to get up." This is the point at which the Strangeness Within collides with the Strangeness Without. The sleep-dazed narrator has the last word, his question pregnant with meaning: "what time is it?" (A question that resonates with the track of that title on the first *Word Jazz* LP.)

The same question is posed (by the second voice) in "Infinite O'Clock." As the title suggests, this hallucinatory piece (cast as quatrains) concerns the quest for the moment outside of time, the eternal moment "beyond the quick and slow" of terrestrial time. The symbol of such a moment is, for the narrator, a half-remembered, mysterious woman, whom he names "the lady from some other place." To re-find her would be to dwell forever where it is "infinite o'clock." As the narrator's voices pronounces the poem, the second voice seems at first to mock and tease, but later comes to enrich the narrator's poem with citations from or allusions to other poems that have as their subject time, mortality or the quest for a mysterious lost female figure. These include *The Rubaiyat of Omar Khayyam,* Shakespeare's "Sonnet 73," John Keats's "La Belle Dame Sans Merci" and E.A. Poe's "To Helen." Both voices are set against the urgent ticking of a clock and the solemn sound of bells tolling the hours, calling to mind our brief time-bound lives and the gulf between our deepest desires and the recalcitrant nature of the material-temporal world we inhabit.

As noisy, boozy New Year's Eve celebrations take place throughout the city around him, the narrator of "The Bub" retreats into isolation, insulating himself from the world's welter within an imaginary protective space he calls "the bubble." For companionship, he conjures his alter ego in whom he confides his "inappropriate thoughts," which comprise a series of outré enterprises he would like to undertake, such as tattoos composed of "slippery ink" that would travel the body, a book consisting of crumpled pages, and a musical starring Siamese twins. The narrator's aspiration, he confides to himself, is to become a "devout catalyst," aloof from all surrounding influences while secretly, subtly exerting his own influence by means of his eccentric projects. These would seem to have as their common denominator the goal of breaking up the given, discomposing the complacent and releasing new possibilities and potentials.

How then is the external, spatio-temporal, material world depicted in *Triple Talk*? What set of conditions provokes so many Nordine protagonists to recoil from or seek to subvert or to transcend ordinary actuality? Apart, of course, from the essential unsatisfactoriness and unpleasant inevitabilities of the mortal human condition, the world at which we each peer from concealment within our separate selves – the Weirdness Without – is here portrayed as a realm of monstrous egotism, petty aggression and devotion to the pursuit of riches, a world characterized by complacency, indifference, futility, and the terrifying prospect of all-annihilating nuclear war.

In "Movie Idea," a brief dialogue in a coffee shop between a script writer and a prominent film star lays bare the limitless vanity to which humans are susceptible. The script writer, who is blatantly sycophantic in his attitude to the star, proposes to the actor a film in which he alone would enact all the roles, play all the characters, that of the lead as well as those of all the supporting actors and actresses, even the extras. The ego-driven actor (initially aloof and dismissive in his dealings with an inferior) relishes the idea, chuckling in self-approbation. Multiplying oneself to the exclusion of everyone else: the ultimate ego fulfilment. As listeners, we are, of course, dismayed to discern the naked and insatiable infantile neediness at the core of such conceit and to contemplate the varied forms that similarly inflated self-worth takes in the world around us.

While the unorthodox ideas of an individual such as "the devout catalyst" of "The Bub" would among most people be considered as uncomfortably and unacceptably bizarre, the world accepts as ordinary and customary certain attitudes and behaviors that ought to be regarded as abnormal. "Bickering" inquires into the preposterous and pernicious practices of common, ordinary people, focusing on the custom of petty quarrelling over trivial issues. The instances cited by the narrator of this track are those of cutting into a neat square of butter from the "wrong" end and positioning toilet paper on the wooden roll in a clockwise (instead of counter clockwise) fashion. The narrator notes that bickering can be perversely pleasurable and that, accordingly, in deliberately defying his wife's preferences in some small matters he is, in fact, doing her a kind of favor: giving her something trivial to rail against. Clearly, upon reflection, such behaviour – while common and acceptable – is truly bizarre and bespeaks a sad kind of jostling and jousting between egos. Bickering over trifles may also represent an unconscious strategy for eluding or deflecting attention from essential existential questions.

"Movers and Shakers" is a biting assessment of "those people who more than anyone else determine what's going to happen, who get things done, who call the shots, who make a big difference." The first two voices heard on the track are those of promoters, arguing for the necessity of raising large amounts of money in order to foster the arts, arguing, of course, for their own lucrative indispensability. The voices of both promoters are tinged with that timbre of self-serving insincerity associated with pitchmen, touts and carnival barkers. A third voice, casual but authoritative, is that of a government official or general, calmly appraising the relative nuclear capabilities of the United States and the Soviet Union. His is a voice embodying, we may say, the ultimate, the most powerful of the breed of movers and shakers, the voice of a true world-shaker. Behind the three foregrounded voices, throughout the track, there is a chorus of voices repeating the phrase "movers and shakers," patently savoring the concept, making vocal genuflections to it, fairly drooling with admiration for the "movers and shakers" of our earth and its inhabitants.

"Mister City" traces to its source the phenomenon of crime in the world, asserting the universality of guilt. "Crime," the voice of the figure of Mister City proclaims, "begins in the heart, crime is a heart disease and you can catch it so easily … I caught it from you, you caught it from her, she caught it from him." The epidemic of sin, it is implied, began in the Garden of Eden. "It happens in gardens," Mister City states, then proceeds to munch an apple. In the end, according to Mister City, we are all "guilty as sin," citizens of the City of Destruction. [40] Additional Biblical references in the track occur as a heckler in the audience asks "am I my brother's keeper?" and another voice recounts an anecdote of a judge who was incensed by being asked the meaning of the phrase "Judge not." (An allusion to the Gospel of Matthew: "Judge not; that ye be not judged. For with what judgement ye judge, ye shall be judged.") Wondering at the world's wickedness, "Mister City" seems to suggest, we might begin by examining our own hearts.

Triple Talk concludes with a self-deflating, serio-comic track titled "Beer and a Shot," combining both poetry and a playlet. The frame of the brief aural drama is that of a man (later identified as Ken Nordine) entering a bar and ordering a beer and a shot from the bartender. After a few sips of his drinks, the man begins to recite a gloomy poem he has composed, rhymed verses concerning the cunning and deceit of the world's powerful, the dubious nature of all systems and of history as written, and the faults and flaws inherent in human nature. The bartender is much discomfited by the man's monologue, insulting him – " are you some kind of poet-nut or something?" – and soon finding an excuse to leave him sitting alone at the bar. Later, upon returning to his duties, the bartender cautions the still declaiming customer: "Uh sir, we don't like people talking to themselves in the bar." Oblivious to disapproval, the poet merely orders another drink. At this point, there is a phone call to the bar and someone, answering the phone, calls out "is there a Ken Nordine here?" Nordine acknowledges his identity and then converses by telephone with his wife, promising to come home presently.

The track is clearly self-deprecatory, Nordine presents himself as a barroom bore, a self-indulgent and somewhat ludicrous prophet of doom who only succeeds in making a nuisance of himself. His lamentations in verse will neither convince anyone of the truth of his grievances nor affect to the smallest degree the world of wrongs he rightly decries. There is a fine ironic pathos in this self-analytical, self-critical presentation. Yet, as a rebuttal to the charges Nordine brings against himself, the very existence of *Triple Talk* evinces a resigned resolve – in the face of absurdity and futility – to keep blowing word jazz to the world.

And, to be sure, further soaring choruses of word jazz are duly blown on *Devout Catalyst* with Nordine swinging, riffing, grooving and playing the changes as once again he navigates his way through the ordinary weirdness of our lives and times. [41] The album contains fresh and fertile musical collaborations with Jerry Garcia and David Grisman and innovative verbal collaborations with Tom Waits. The core themes of the album are, however, a clear extension of Nordine's abiding concerns: our world, our selves, and the reciprocal actions and influences between the two.

Unbridled greed and insatiable egotism are selected as themes in "Mr. Slick," and "Zodiac Uprising." The former is a portrait in rhymed run-on couplets of a shameless hustler working in the entertainment industry, exploiting his audience's appetite for titillation, vulgarizing the classics for profit, repeating again and again shallow commercially successful film formulae. As his name indicates, Mr. Slick is the embodiment of all that is slippery, tricky, shrewd and superficial, and – alas – all too frequently "successful" in our world. There may, perhaps, be a suggestion on this track that those qualities represented by Mr. Slick constitute a modern manifestation of original sin. At the outset, he is likened to a snake "sliding on a bellyache" (curable only by money, as we are later apprised), and an ally and benefactor of Mr. Slick, we are told, is "the guy who owns the money tree." These may be allusions to imagery in Genesis, but of this I'm unsure.

"Zodiac Uprising," a dramatic dialogue with sound effects, tells the story of a near-future society where private ownership has been extended to include the very stars in the night sky. The stars have been marketed and sold to various moneyed individuals, who on the basis of official deeds of ownership then lay claim to these celestial bodies in what can only be seen as an unconscionable act of self-aggrandizement. A reaction to this injustice is a clandestine uprising, consisting of various allied astrological factions such as the Aries Faction and eleven others. These aggrieved groups have – like ancient Christians meeting in the catacombs – taken to meeting in the sewers to foment rebellion. A critique of class privilege and power relations, the track also takes aim at social delusion and self-deception. For clearly, the entire premise of marketing the stars is a fraud. No government or institution can, of course, honestly or sanely assert possession of the heavens and thus have the right to sell individual stars. Accordingly, it would be foolish and self-deceiving for purchasers to imagine that with the acquisition of an official deed they could claim ownership of a star or stars. Since such proprietorship is no more than fanciful, in reality then nothing has been gained or lost by the sale or purchase of stars and there is, therefore, no real cause for resentment and rebellion on the part of the have-nots. "Zodiac Uprising" reminds us of our collective folly in devoting so much of our lives to coveting mirages, bartering shadows, pursuing phantoms, hankering after the sham and the bogus, seduced and deluded by illusions, all the while neglecting what is real and true and vital in life.

The absurd, pathetic – often desperate – drive for material acquisition and to attain status and prestige may be seen as an unconscious endeavor on the part of an individual to seek in trivial gains and satisfactions some assurance of importance or safety, an attempt to assuage an inner wound, to fill a vast inner void. But soon or late the individual so engaged learns that the anguish of emptiness leaks through, breaks through, pervading the mind of the evader. We witness this sad condition among the patrons of a bar called "Is" in the track titled "Inside of Is." Superficially exuberant and mirthful, each person present there is secretly alone and afraid. Each patron, we are told, bears "a hidden scar," and dissimulates a fear of running out of time, "running out of breath." In the interim, there is distraction in the form of lust, alcohol, rants, laughter, obsession and contrived eccentricity. As if in testimony to their false, shallow, social selves, none is called by a proper name but instead known only by grotesque nicknames: Scrambled Eggs, Skinny, Soup Bone, Door Knob and Sister Sideways. For all their desperate efforts to seize the "is" of time, to hide forever in the present instant, the narrator tells us that even inside Is "stuff can happen very fast / future changes into past." Time is ineluctable, inexorable; ultimately the interior emptiness can no longer be contained, ultimately that emptiness must meet and merge with nothingness. The joke told early in the track about the pig becoming reduced to chops, ribs and pickled knuckles serves to foreshadow their final end. If there is sanctuary and safety to be found somewhere, it is not inside "is," it is elsewhere, in an unexplored region beyond the social mask and the craving ego.

If the pitiful patrons of "Is" strive to evade awareness, the narrator of "Quatrains of Thought" attempts to engage with the essential existential questions. "Wonder where I'm going," the narrator of the track asks himself, "don't know where I've been / On my way to somewhere." The title of the track – an interior monologue formed in quatrains – is a pun on the phrase "train of thought," and the image of a moving train with stations and stops is central to the lyric.

The narrator of "Quatrains of Thought" seems to be alone, riding a train, watching the passing stations, watching the rain drops clinging to the windows of the moving train, brooding, musing, melancholy. The train stations recall to his mind memories of significant events in his life: mistakes, disappointments, deadends, confusions, fears. The forward movement of the train toward its end station suggests to him a metaphor for his life: the startling way his life seemed suddenly to accelerate, yet how wearily long the journey sometimes seems, and always and ever the final destination nearer and nearer. He regrets never having attained to a comprehensive vision of life, its purpose, its meaning, ("never been to Total") and wonders whether antidepressants might still his disquiet. Finally, he speculates as to the fate of the spirit after death: what if God is indifferent to us, what if the spirit finds itself forever lost and alone in infinite darkness? All these questions and tensions are left unresolved. Nordine's solitary passenger may be seen as an Everyman, his situation a concise depiction of the human condition in all its "thrownness," its insecurity and uncertainty.

Another embodiment of Everyman is the "Aging Young Rebel" called "Whatshisname." Wishing to distinguish himself from the mass of humankind, wishing to challenge and change the world, he undergoes a fearful journey to final selfhood. Like John Bunyan's pilgrim, Christian,

Whatshisname   encounters allegorical personifications called Clever, Cunning, Diabolical and Gentle. He is told by some that he must be mad and told by others that his ideals are hopeless. Fleeing confusion and discouragement, he is ambushed by Diabolical to whom he loses a foot, whereafter he contemplates suicide, but is rescued by Gentle, who in cruel kindness amputates his other foot, thus symbolically restoring balance and proportion. This nightmare parable in verse ends with a pitiless pun: Whathisname is now "footless and fancy free." After an initial shock at this seemingly savage bit of word play, we realize that while his body is disabled, his spirit is enabled; he is, at once, maimed and made whole. The phrase "fancy free" means free to imagine or think as one pleases, free from restraint. For Whatshisname (as, indeed, for everyone) suffering and loss would seem to be the awful cost of coming to a fuller understanding of the world, of achieving individual freedom and autonomy.

Resonating with "Quatrains of Thought," and with "Aging Young Rebel," the final track on *Devout Catalyst,* titled "Last Will," cast in rough doggerel, treats of life's vanities: the voracious greed of some, our failure to see beneath the surface of things, our elaborate disguises, our profitless projects, our unkept promises, neglected obligations and unrealized dreams, our futile pursuits: "forgotten locks to doors that once were trees." Again, human life is viewed here as cruel and confusing and death as its inevitable end. This solemn meditation on avarice, dereliction and mortality is not, however, without a note of metaphysical hope. The narrator finds solace in the thought that "the maker of it all has tricks up every sleeve." Despite our many misgivings and apprehensions, then, despite our incomprehension, there still abides somewhere in the spirit an instinct of trust.

A track titled "Thousand Bing Bangs" – a duet with Tom Waits – is among Nordine's most experimental. To the musical accompaniment of Garcia and Grisman, Waits and Nordine alternate speaking separate, unrelated narratives. Waits tells the surreal tale of an extremely eccentric (not to say outré) woman he knew long ago while Nordine delivers nervous reflections on identity and consciousness. The collision of recitals, defiantly disorderly, resists coherence. I think, perhaps, that may be the point here: we each inhabit our own entirely subjective reality, convinced of the validity of our own perceptions, believing that our personal illusions correspond to objective reality. *Devout Catalyst* also features versions of "Cracks in the Ceiling" and "The Final Page," and a track called "I Love a Groove" which celebrates the benign power of music to lift our spirits and to synchronize our erratic lives with the vitalizing rhythms of Life.

Further uniquely Nordinesque incursions into the bewilderness of contemporary social norms, mores and psychological states, mixed with a few unsettling reflections on certain phenomena of the physical world, and some more optimistic metaphysical musings, make up Ken Nordine's next album, *A Transparent Mask*. [42] The twenty tracks comprising the album can be seen as divided among those expressing perplexity or dread in the face of existence, those treating of human weakness and those affirming what is held by Nordine to be worthy of attention or furtherance in our all-too-real, surreal world.

Among those few things worth pursuing through all this dense weirdness in which we blunder about, Nordine contends, is love. Four tracks on *A Transparent Mask* take as their topic one or another aspect of human love: "You Know the Story," "You Don't Love Me Blues," "You Were So Crazy" and "What's There to Do." The first of these portrays the uncertainties, hesitations, complexities, tensions and giddy joys of courtship. We may all be "dirty as mud, heavy with ego," but love can transform us, the narrator of this poem asserts, so that we "glide" and "shimmer" and ascend to a state of interpersonal unity that partakes of divinity. Unrequited love, however, can cause us relentless distress, as expressed in the "You Don't Love Me Blues." Even love experienced long ago in youth can still when recollected in old age evoke pangs of loss as when the first person narrator of "You Were So Crazy" finds himself haunted by the memory of a fleeting instant from the distant past: "all you see is her falling hair." The final track on the album, "What's There To Do," another love lyric, confirms the sovereign power of love, here depicted as the sustaining bedrock foundation of all that is of value and significance in human life.

It may be unclear to us, though, whether love is to be considered as a state-of-spirit that accords with the essential nature of the universe or whether love is a hard-won, anomalous, uncertain victory in a world that is fundamentally and finally dark and cruel. For it is plain that selfish appetite or predation is principal among Creation's laws. This argument is implicit in "Cat and Bird Blues," where the primary relationship animating the natural world is presented as that of hunter and prey: cat and bird. From such primal ferocity our spirits recoil and in desperation we implore: "where's the golden door?" How do we get out of here? How can we break free from the terror at the heart of the natural world and attain a higher realm of being? "A Good Year for Spiders" extends the motif of predation (spider heaven as "one infinite snare") while "For the Birds," though rendering again a world of peril and death, mutability and loss – "this shifting insubstantial everywhere" – yet affirms a calm, cosmic acceptance and assurance, citing in the end Hamlet's pronouncement "there's a special providence in the fall of a sparrow." [43] The title of the track is a pun, suggesting that this world is "for the birds," that is to say worthless, no good, useless and futile, and suggesting also that the track is an ode addressed to and in praise of birds, employing the bird image as a metaphor for human life and fate. Shakespeare employs the same metaphor in Hamlet's speech cited above, arguing that every life, every destiny – from that of a humble sparrow to that of a prince – is under God's governance.

In human beings predatory behavior can take many forms, the common denominator of which is assertive egotism. This mode of perceiving and acting is epitomized in "Hole in the Ego," the tale of a man who from the hour of his birth is insatiable in his craving for attention and other forms of gratification. The track titled "The Guru" represents a less extreme form of egotism but one rich in irony as a guru is, of course, supposed to have transcended ego-consciousness and liberated himself from desires and attachments. This particular guru, however, is revealed as a "slippery shaman," a deceiver secretly seeking pre-eminence and power, feeding off the esteem of gullible devotees. Several degrees lower on the scale of egotism but still registering an appreciable level of egocentricity is the narrator of "A Thousand Dreams," who desires complete success – romantic and economic – complete validation, unqualified approval and acclaim.

In contradistinction to the self-centred, self-serving predators and megalomaniacs, there are the edgy, existential, introspective, neurotic, somewhat bewildered individuals so often the heroes of Nordine's tales and dramas. These are uneasy, unreconciled persons, struggling to attain or maintain some kind of foothold in reality, endeavoring to achieve some measure of security, even as they are assailed by angst, doubt, solitude or insomnia. We encounter such a protagonist in "Hello," an anonymous voice, someone, somewhere, seemingly alone in a void, a lonely soul, urgently seeking contact with someone else. He once knew someone, he says aloud to the void, who collected hellos, someone like himself, seeking human contact, however fleeting and distant. The protagonist admits that like that mad collector, he is himself sustained by "certain kinds of going mad." We are left to infer what extremes of loneliness or mental anguish can be mitigated only by madness. In "A Thousand Bingbangs," another such protagonist, having found himself "ravelled" and "gone out of focus" in a world of getting and spending, climbing and striving, has turned his back on what he characterizes as "operas of mock and mumble, comedies of who-you-know," and (like the other damaged protagonists) has taken refuge in a self-created realm of fancy, a small, frail psychic bubble adrift in a cold and ever-expanding universe.

Another refugee from reality finds a personal sanctuary in "Cliché Heaven," an imaginary domain of his own devising where a comforting risk-free banality and predictability prevail. In "Truth Mute," what is apparently an interior voice (distant, distorted, originating from somewhere deep within the psyche) makes contact with the sleeping mind of the exterior personality, interrupting the sleeper's unconscious state in order to impart to him disturbing occasions of fear and disquiet as experienced by the interior voice. The voice describes feeling trapped in dreams over which he has no control and a distressing sense of dissociation and derealization. The voice admits to seeking reassurance in lies and delusions and expresses a wish for "a truth mute," a device that would serve to dampen and diminish the reception of the raw realities of the exterior world, making conscious (or unconscious) awareness more bearable. Common to all these angst-ridden individuals is a desire to escape from the physical world with all its griefs and vexations, a wistful aspiration to exist somewhere at the further side of time. Beyond, however, the tentative relief obtained by them in certain forms of madness and imagination, their unfortunate situations (essentially the human condition) would seem to be irresolvable.

It is, as we have seen, in human love and in faith (the sense of "a special providence" guiding all) that Nordine suggests a true course may be discerned in life's vast baffling labyrinth. Also helpful along the way are certain other hints and glints of meaning, including those discovered by physics and mathematics or those derived from pondering a familiar topic. Among such instances on *A Transparent Mask* are "As of Now," "Quarks" and "Fibonacci Numbers." In the first of these the topic is the sheer strangeness of time, its arbitrary and subjective measurements, the unaccountable simultaneous occurrence of beginnings and endings, the passage of time as a progression of fleeting, elusive, irretrievable "nows." Though we live our lives in time, taking time for granted, it remains an incomprehensible mind-bending mystery, which to contemplate can awaken in us a self-transcending awe.

Surpassingly strange, too, are phenomena such as the subatomic particles known as quarks, "a hypothetical entity ... there somewhere inside the basic constituents of matter." Again, to reflect on so ultimately unfathomable a topic is to be teased out of "the pigeon holes of our minds," as Nordine says, to be confronted with a dizzying mystery that disrupts ordinary consciousness and takes us beyond ourselves. Significantly, these infinitely small entities have been classified as "T" or "truth quarks" and "B" or "beauty quarks," leading Nordine to cite the concluding lines of John Keats' poem, "Ode to a Grecian Urn," (1820): "Beauty is truth, truth beauty, that is all ye know on earth, and all ye need to know." The allusion to Keats seems to suggest a view that the utmost truth and beauty of the universe will ever elude the grasp of our intellects and that long before atomic physicists theorized the presence of such strangeness and mystery, the poets had, so to speak, already been there.

No less curious than quarks are Fibonacci numbers, named for Leonardo Pisano Bogollo, called "Fibonacci," (1170-1250.) In conversation with himself, Nordine discusses the discovery of what is known as by mathematicians as the "Fibonacci Sequence," a series of numbers formed by adding together the two previous numbers in the sequence. While apparently discovered by Fibonacci on a whim, out of sheer inquisitive curiosity, a discovery of no obvious practical relevance or application, the Fibonacci Sequence proves to have, as Nordine states, "very surprising relations to botany and classical art." The numerical ratios that characterize Fibonacci Numbers are found to occur naturally in the patterns of seashells, flower petals, pine cones, pineapples, the arrangement of leaves, the branching of trees and elsewhere, as well as corresponding to classical theories of beauty and proportion (the Golden Ratio) and pitch relations in music. Some have called the sequence "nature's secret code," "nature's universal rule" and "God's own creation equation." We are reminded once again of the value of a sense of possibility and uncertainty, the value of whimsy and imagination as conceptual tools, and reminded, too, of the presence of an elusive mystery at the heart of things, a mystery underlying and permeating the world.

Whatever the prevalence in our world of error and terror, then, there is also beauty and mystery, and love and humor. This hardwon premise supports a further series of observations – keen, oblique, deft, apt, droll and rueful – collected on *Grandson of Word Jazz*. [44] Side one of the album consists of a suite of poems titled "The Seasons," depicting the changing weathers and moods of the calendar-based year. The narrator, having known the seasons and seen the annual cycles of growth and diminution through many repetitions, has come to see the ending as already implicit in the beginning: "I see the winter begin in the spring." He is, he states, well-acquainted with "old zero," the silence, the stillness of spirit, the sombre thoughts that come with winter and has become alert to all the portents of winter that can occur even in the exuberances of early springtime: "you knew it would happen." Indeed, even as life awakens and flowers bloom and the spring gains ground, he feels the ghosts of winter clutching him still, pulling him back, reminding him that spring is no more than a prelude to winter. Then at last there comes at an hour in high summer when the summer season can seem invincible and "fall is just a myth." Inevitably, though, the old earth "wobbles and tilts," and autumn returns and with it the realization that once more you have allowed yourself to be deceived. And now you learn yet once more that nothing lasts, that all is provisional, all is transient, that time is inexorable and all that survives, all that can be saved is the eternal moment of human love.

The reverse side of the album consists of a diverse series of sketches and songs, employing voice distortions, sound effects (marching feet, musketry, explosions, cheering crowd, applause) and musical accompaniment. The first track, titled "Calico Blues," begins with a prologue in the form of a conversation between two friends, one of whom aspires to open a store-front café or club that he would call "Free Lessons." In the window he would place a little rock, a single silk acetate sock and a sign reading "19 cents." This playfully quaint notion puts me in mind of the Karesansui or Japanese dry landscape garden associated with Zen Buddhism. Nordine's version of a particular selection and arrangement of objects for his window display seems to me an expression of the very zaniest of Zen arts, a zenith of Zen. It is also an example of hip absurdist humour of the kind reflected in names such as "The Co-Existence Bagel Shop," "The Abomunist Manifesto" and "The Happy Birthday of Death." [45]

"Calico Blues" takes off as a harmonica wails and Nordine chants a blues, while a second voice reacts with approval and appreciation. The text of the song concerns the enigma of existence: "Everywhere I look I see the puzzle/more you work it, the funnier it gets/ every piece you see is supposed to fit in/could it be that Mr. Puzzle just forgets?/think of all the thinking that's been forgot/pieces of the puzzle that get lost/see, I thought I had this little corner almost finished/gotta work it out at any cost/could it be that the puzzle's getting larger/quick as we can fill the pieces in?/the more you know the larger the unknown becomes." Part of the puzzle, the singer relates, is his calico cat, so handsome, so charming, and so deadly a hunter, so pitiless a killer of birds. In essence, this lyrical anecdote illustrates what is termed by theologians "the problem of evil," that is the paradox of the existence of evil and suffering in a world created by an omnipotent and benevolent deity. There are, of course, a myriad of disquisitions on this mystery. Nordine attempts no resolution in "Calico Blues," but acknowledges that the dreadful appetite of his beloved cat is "part of the puzzle," the bewildering metaphysical riddle he is engaged in trying to solve. He may have found as yet no definitive answers, no certainties, but he is no less curious about the nature of existence and still concerned to solve at least some little corner of the great puzzle.

The motif of the puzzle is repeated in the track that follows, titled "The Swami." A pilgrim in search of "the true and only way" approaches a swami, who can only convey his wisdom to the seeker in terms of a kind of *koan:* "the true and only way is in front of you when your back is turned." Protesting that the swami speaks in puzzles, the seeker is told by him: "everyone speaks in puzzles." Is the implication here that there is inevitably an element of deception or distortion at the heart of our systems of language? Or is this merely an excuse for obfuscation? In a comic reversal of the customary roles, the seeker enlightens the swami by playing musical sounds on the Jew's harp, raising the swami to a state of ecstasy and moving him to pronounce "it is the truth." But if even the simplest of musical sounds can sometimes resonate with the spirit, music can also be reduced to banality and blandness, as in "Cuz You're So," a parody of clichéd pop tunes and their trivial lyrics: "you've been to silly/you've been to dumb/you know just where I'm coming from." Implicitly, "Cuz You're So" poses questions concerning the hyper-commercialization of popular music and the deleterious effect on the listening audience of such vacuous, formulaic aural froth and fluff.

"Feet of Clay" recounts in the form of a sketch and a song the brief life of an aspirationally upwardly mobile optimist who comes to an untimely end, executed by a firing squad. Even unto the final seconds of his life he seems to maintain the belief that his imminent demise is only a temporary setback that can be overcome with some glib talk and glad-handing. His life has been characterized by naïve dreams of wealth. He liked to think, we are told, that "something metal could be zinc." At the same time, he sought to align himself with "the middle," to find sanctuary among the group. His opportunistic optimism combined with his careful conformity proved in the end to be "feet of clay." Having ignored and neglected the essentials in life, in the end he achieved neither wealth nor safety.

A similarly sad case is that of "Charlie Bingbang," who, having first withdrawn into himself, ends as a friendless suicide. Jumping from a tall building, his descent re-enacts, we are told, the Fall of Man, perhaps in the sense that he has somehow lost both innocence and faith. Criticism, the lyrics inform us, was his goal in life. Perhaps the black beam of negativity was ultimately turned on himself and he could not bear what he beheld in that pitiless light. His flaw seems to have been of an opposite but complementary kind to that of the man with feet of clay: an excess of negativity as opposed to an excess of optimism.

The final track on *Grandson of Word Jazz*, -- "What's So Funny?" – is a self-mocking piece in the manner of "Beer and a Shot" on *Triple Talk*, but one that is far more complex. Nordine first assumes the persona of a self-savoring entertainer basking in the cheering adulation of his audience, proclaiming with false modesty that "I never thought I'd wind up here," thanking his business agent, thanking the crowd "for just being you," and thanking us for listening to the record, urging us to tell our friends about it (so that they, too, will purchase the album.) Not only does Nordine pretend on this track to be a pompous, insincere, self-serving charlatan but when his routine is ended we hear Nordine as voice actor (no longer playing the role) chortle with pleasure at his own performance. We then hear a third voice – also that of Nordine, i.e. another Nordine – remark with some annoyance: "What's so funny?" In effect, then, there are three distinct (but not separate) voices or identities corresponding to three levels of (un)reality: Nordine the voice actor creates a parodic version of himself, then Nordine in the role of himself as actor expresses satisfaction with his own performance in satirizing himself, and, finally, Nordine the observer of the voice actor identity comments disapprovingly on his own self-approval. The piece comprises a kind of meta-parody, ending the album in a comic jumble of collapsed identities and realities.

Ken Nordine's most recent compilation of quirky words set to the angular rhythms of his singular brain waves is *Bits & Pieces of Word Jazz*. [46] The title suggests a kind of miscellany or omnium-gatherum but – like its predecessors – *Bits and Pieces* (the title may be a pun on short theatrical routines and literary or dramatic compositions) is a varied but cohesive collection, restating and reinforcing essential themes of the word jazz series. A unifying image implicit or explicit on many pieces on the album is that of a cage, a metaphor for those forces, circumstances, habits, appetites or attitudes that serve to confine or constrain the mind or the spirit.

The seemingly most capacious but ultimately hermetic and unyielding of such cages is that of the human condition, our mortality, our situation within temporal limits. In "Tick Tock Talk" Nordine treats once again the theme of time, the relentless swiftness of its passing, the radical contingency and sad ephemerality of our lives in time. Time, the poet-speaker perceives, is the trap in which we are caught, the snare in which we are entangled, the quicksand in which we are quickly sinking. "What's the time of anywhere?" the poem asks, but the answer was given already in the first line: always and ever, everywhere and everywhen the time is "once within much later on close to very soon." So flickering, so fleeting, so sudden, so thin is ever-running time.

In "No News is Good News Blues," human existence is imaged variously as a "maze," a "fix," a "trap," a "forest" in which we are lost. We find ourselves in a hazardous realm of mutual devouring – birds, mosquitoes, cats, mice – where we are surrounded by "enemies," and even ambushed from inside ourselves by "enemies within us." Raddled and uncertain, we seek orientation and understanding, but the only constants in our harried lives are (in Kierkegaard's phrase) *fear and trembling*: "worry is eternal/same is true of fear." And so we hide, camouflage ourselves, lying low, taking bleak comfort in the adage that "no news is good news," and finding our only solace in forming out of our misfortunes a blues, attaining in this way a momentary victory over our fate, a short-lived but triumphant secular salvation.

A similar grief informs "Moments with Father Time," a long lamentation enumerating the afflictions and tribulations inherent in the human condition. The narrator views his life as but a "speck of whirling dust" in an "incomprehensible" and entropic universe. In an overpopulated world, his ego-schemes and ideas are no more than "a sack of sweet nonsense." And even as the narrator laments and repents, he is aware that the present instant of conscious existence is constantly "slipping away," with time-past encroaching second by second upon an ever-moving present, the actual moment escaping us even as we scurry to stay abreast of it. We feel haunted and thwarted by a sense that there may be a saving insight just beyond our reach and by the feeling that no sooner do we almost grasp "some mumble of insight," than like a ghost it dissipates and vanishes before our baffled brains. Vainly, "we look for the map," we seek to find the "plot" of our lives or to impose one, all the while straining to maintain a brave face, a smiling social mask. We pray to God for forgiveness, we plead, but secretly we fear that in the Court of Divine Justice "pleas for mercy aren't heard," and that "God is stone deaf in Plea Bargain Heaven." Perhaps, though, a model of right living is to be found in "some bird who sings without lessons," bravely making music in spite of "the weight of right now." And perhaps, after all, there may be some grace and spiritual refreshment to be obtained – not in philosophy, not in theology, not in contriving to have an "agenda" or assuming a "mask," not in "slurring our grieving" with drink – but in simple, innocent trust, as when parched plants complain to the heavens of draught and are answered with rain that seeps down to quicken their deepest roots.

The perilous prevalence of cages of all kinds (temporal, psychological, social, conceptual, ontological) is asserted in the short, potent, declarative sentence (a citation from Franz Kafka's *The Zurau Aphorisms)* that provides both title and lyric for the track "A Cage Went in Search of a Bird." [47] The phrase seems to suggest that the agencies of constriction and confinement in this world are relentless in their aim of curtailing freedom, actively seeking out instances of freedom (for which the bird serves as metaphor) in order to repress and constrain it. This same restrictive force or principle is denounced in "Collecting My Thoughts," where "strait-laced thinking," mental corsets and collars, are seen as the deadly antithesis of free thought and creative imagination. An internalized fear among some people of "inappropriate thoughts" is seen to lead to a form of self-censorship and to promote stifling conformity. Some people, the narrator avers, even come to savor the constraint to which they are subject, renouncing altogether the "vagrant spirit" which might otherwise deliver them from spiritual and emotional sterility.

Another invisible cage confining the human spirit is that of consumerism, as treated by Nordine in the tracks "Credit Card Blues" and "So Many Things." The former piece satirizes the culture of consumption with its insidious appeal to the immediate gratification of artificial desires. Unable to afford the products that they imagine will alleviate boredom, confer distinction upon them, embellish their lives or grant them happiness, would-be consumers are encouraged by banks and advertisers to purchase on credit the goods they covet. In this way, they enter the consumer treadmill: their purchases quickly lose their promised magic meaning and they are left feeling empty, while their anxieties are heightened by their increasing indebtedness. They are thus driven to consume more in a futile not to say febrile search for satisfaction and a vain effort to allay their mounting economic distress, even as they incur more debt.

In "Credit Card Blues," Nordine assumes the persona of a slick tempter, a kind of hip huckster urging self-indulgence, commending credit-financed consumption: "get yourself some plastic, have yourself a spree, you can pay up later." The consequences of a preoccupation with possessions are considered in "So Many Things," which begins with the premise: "so many things you want to buy, so many things you want to get." But in order to obtain the material goods to which you aspire you will, of course, be obliged to find suitable employment. This will, Nordine argues, necessitate changing your appearance to conform with the standards and expectations of prospective employers, making a good impression at interviews, perhaps cultivating others to make "the right connections," agreeing to accede to all the requirements of the job including working on weekends, submitting to IQ measurements and a host of other intrusive demands. The point of this track is to make us aware of how much of our individuality we forfeit in order to fulfil our material aspirations. Taking the bait, we ensnare ourselves, incarcerating ourselves in perpetuity within a cage of our own making.

Against all the fell forces arrayed against the human spirit – the meshes of time and matter, the dreadful voracity of living organisms, an all-pervasive commercialism, insidious social conformity and corporate regimentation, narrow prescriptive morality, rigid ideologies and orthodoxies, existential anxiety, and the seductions of consumerism – is a profound, persistent intuition trembling ever at the verge of revelation, that there is some salvatory insight – as proposed in "Moments with Father Time" – ever beckoning just beyond the grasp of our understanding. That same track also makes an allusion to Plato's allegory of the cave suggesting that like the prisoners in Plato's cave we, too, are confined to a world of illusions. Beyond the cave (our conceptual cage) is the realm of the real and the true. Although, like Plato's prisoners, we are deceived by shadows we yet sense (and sometimes glimpse) the presence of a higher reality beyond the material-temporal world. Responding to such intimations, we pray to God for deliverance from time: "tell us heaven's there/tell us things go on and on/ ... wind us up forevermore." We seek an exit from this brutal place in which we are confined: "Where's the golden door?" ("No News is Good News Blues," echoing a similar cry in "Cat and Bird Blues" on *A Transparent Mask.)* We take refuge in the belief or hope that "there's a special providence in the fall of a sparrow," as cited (again, see "For the Birds" on *A Transparent Mask*) at the end of the track "A Cage Went in Search of a Bird." And like the parched gardens in "No News is Good News Blues," we wait for rain from the heavens to revive our stricken roots. These are, to be sure, heavy matters, but handled – as ever by Nordine – with a light touch, with wit and with an original and individual sense of the absurd. The associative leaps and dreamlike links of words generate a sense of mystery, taking the edge off what can sometimes seem rather a dark vision – or at least a dim view – of things.

In addition to the several word jazz albums discussed above, there is a further body of word jazz performances by Ken Nordine in the form of radio broadcasts. From the 1970s through the 1980s, Nordine wrote, produced and performed weekly shows for National Public Radio: a first series titled "Now, Nordine," and a second series called "Ken Nordine's Word Jazz." Episodes of these broadcasts – which share the satirical spirit and surreal ethos of the word jazz recordings – number in the hundreds.

Each half-hour show is an avalanche of strangeness, a collage of craziness, a mad mix of words and sounds, an auditory hallucination. Typically, a "Now, Nordine" show begins with a parody of the customary NPR announcement of corporate sponsorship of individual programs, as Ken Nordine solemnly states: "the following program is made possible by a grant from anonymous." The show then commences with a monologue or a skit a few minutes in length, after which to the accompaniment of a deep ominous musical tone, Nordine pronounces: "As you listen to the following, for your imagination's sake turn off the lights if it's dark out or close your eyes if it's light – unless you're driving of course – and you'll see as only you can see with that special inner eye you have, with that special insight that makes you differently the same." This is followed by Nordine, with the full confidence and authority of an announcer, uttering the word "now," to which a second voice reacts with alarm: "now what?" "Now, Nordine," is the reply.

"Ken Nordine's Word Jazz," the successor to "Now, Nordine," begins with the sound of a ping pong ball bouncing and a voice furtively hissing "psst." This is immediately followed by a louder voice spelling out the word letter by letter: "p-s-s-t," and asking "are you ready?" "Here it is," the voice continues, "Ken Nordine's Word Jazz, proudly presented by You-Know-Who." After an initial skit of short duration, we hear metallic clanking and a profound, portentous musical tone against which Nordine states: "Word Jazz (yeah) here we are you and I, here we are with something imaginary in the trembling air between us. Where will the imaginary take us this time?" Even as he speaks, in the background other voices chuckle and echo his words.

Apart from these announcements, formally anchoring listeners in a realm of weirdness, the broad-casts are antic, anarchic and completely unpredictable, a succession of diverse and disparate sketches ending abruptly or fading away, interrupted by further sketches which are then displaced in their turn , all to the accompaniment of clucking chickens, buzzing flies, snatches of music or the sounds of explosions. A recurrent feature of the broadcasts is Nordine's use of multiple voices, (all of them his own, of course, recorded over each other in layers) suggesting a kind of "multiphrenia," as he has named it. That is in addition to the main narrative voice there are several other voices commenting, affirming, questioning, going off on tangents of their own, maniacally repeating words and phrases, mocking, heckling, arguing, vying for attention and dominance. The effect is that of being inside a fractionated mind in conflict with itself, each unruly autonomous sub-division of consciousness clamoring to be heard, insisting on its own importance, challenging the prevailing hierarchy of awareness. At the same time, the effect of the disjunctions, juxtapositions and incongruities among and within the separate sketches is that of suggesting multiple simultaneous realities, shifting, wavering, interpenetrating, combining, vanishing, being succeeded by new configurations. In the receptive, responsive listener, there is a condition of mind induced by these broadcasts, in which habitual structures of identity and conventional notions of the real are temporarily suspended, permitting the disclosure of alternative perceptions and conceptions.

The radio shows often include a track from the classic word jazz albums (as well as presenting sketches included on later recordings) but much of the material employed in the broadcasts is of a nature rather more outré than customary even for Nordine. It may be said that in the radio shows Nordine pulls out all the stops and outdoes himself. At various times (to a chorus of taunts and derision from his other voices and against the sounds of horse races and prize fights) Nordine reads aloud from train schedules and bird watching guides, from geography textbooks and Sir James Frazier's *The Golden Bough: A Study of Comparative Religion* (1890), from cookbooks and books on nutrition, from a surgical manual and a medical text on infectious diseases, from a medieval bestiary and from an academic lecture on *Hamlet,* from Aristotle's *Nicomachean Ethics* (Book X) and from Erasmus's *In Praise of Folly* (1509), as well as from a variety of literary works including Jonathan Swift's *Gulliver's Travels* (1726) and Aldous Huxley's *Island* (1962), passages from *Ulysses* (1922) and *Finnegans Wake* (1939) by James Joyce, from "The Grand

Inquisitor" chapter of *The Brothers Karamazov* (1880) by Fyodor Dostoevski, from Søren Kirkegaard's writings, from *The Rubaiyat of Omar Khayyam,* and from poems by William Shakespeare, William Makepiece Thackery, Henry Wadsworth Longfellow, George Pope Morris, A.E. Housman, T.S. Eliot and others. The decontextualization of these texts and their recontextualization among incongruous sound effects and quarrelsome voices serves to elicit in the mind of the listener a sense of the mystery inherent in words and the worlds they evoke, fugitive worlds impinged upon by other fugitive worlds, multiple bubble realities colliding. Or, as Nordine announces at one point: "we interrupt the end of this program to bring you the beginning of the next one."

In the course of these broadcasts, Nordine turns his amazed attention to topics as various as mud, sleep, applause and approval, xerography, numbers, clothes, placebos, minced oaths, politicians, the central nervous system, computer generated music, humility, property values, marriage counselling, vanity, oxygen, lechery, bacilli and time. He satirizes intellectual fads with a sketch on chicken brain implants and satirizes spiritual fads with a sketch on "the oracle," a guru of ultra self-indulgent hedonism. He reads aloud (with growing alarm) from a boxed warning detailing the numerous and dire contraindications of a common over-the-counter medicinal remedy. He engages in a deadpan absurd exchange (an actual recorded telephone conversation) with a telemarketer who is attempting to persuade him to invest in stock. He ponders the baffling relativity of the concepts of "here" and "there." He muses on the mathematics of Andrey Andreyevich Markov (1856-1922). His voice slows down and deepens then speeds up, rising to a falsetto; his accents change from dialects of vernacular American English to R.P. to a succession of foreign accents, his electronically altered voice reaches our ears as if spoken through a telephone or a megaphone. There is an exhilarating sense of spontaneity, of improvisation, of free association. As Nordine has remarked: "When I do a show. I don't know where I'm leading. If you knew where you were leading, sometimes maybe you wouldn't want to go there." [48] These broadcasts are, I believe, to be numbered among the most innovative, the most experimental and the most idiosyncratic in radio history. They are hip, "trippy" and very funny.

Many are the occasions on which Ken Nordine has invited us to stare with our ears as he conducts us through remote inward realms of the imaginary. In his most recent work he invites us to stare with our eyes as well. In 2005, Nordine released a 90 minute DVD titled *The Eye is Never*

Filled: Word Jazz in Morphing Pictures. [49] The DVD consists of thirty word jazz pieces set to musical accompaniment and augmented by abstract computer-generated visuals. Among the tracks, Nordine compositions (drawn from previous collections) predominate, but are supplemented with texts by William Shakespeare, Edward Lear, Eugene Field and Edwin Arlington Robinson. The visuals are essentially hallucinatory, with colors in constant movement, flowing, swirling, taking sinuous shapes, merging, dissolving, forming. Sometimes with reference to the text being performed (as in Nordine's rendering of "The Akond of Swat" which is accompanied by the grim visages of infamous dictators) there are images of human faces made elastic, distorted, stretched to grotesque proportions. More often, though, the undulating colored images are ravishing, ethereal, trance-inducing, a worthy extension of the word jazz mode and further testimony to Nordine's ever-restless, boundary-breaking creative imagination.

Genially deviant, playfully serious, impertinently pertinent, irreverently reverent, gracefully out-of-step, Ken Nordine has for over half a century spoken his piece to whoever has ears to hear. Even among the trailblazing hepcats, misfits and mavericks of the subcultural spoken arts LP, Nordine's work is distinctive, his voice and vision individual. His art has remained infused with a jazz ethos of exploration, invention and discovery, deploying displaced accents and shifting meters of the mind, variable and unpredictable perceptual/conceptual lines, together with a subtly dissident dissonance.

Viewed in perspective across the years, both in manner and in matter, Nordine's word jazz exhibits continuity and expansion. From the earliest tracks it is clear that a central theme of word jazz is opposition to what Nordine sees as a narrow and inadequate concept of human existence, an essential misconception caused by misdirected energies and misemployed attention. Humans are portrayed in Nordine's work as inclined to misspend their lives in pursuit of social status, material gain and empty pleasures, and in so doing denying, ignoring or neglecting the life of the imagination and the life of the spirit. Serving to perpetuate our alienation from intuitions of deeper meaning are the all-pervading, homogenizing forces of mass media, mass marketing and mass entertainment. And further reinforcing a barren status quo are barriers comprised of established forms and norms, preconceptions and certainties, habits and categories, clichés and platitudes, and all that is fixed and static.

Beyond taking incisive digs at the various commercial and techno-social structures that seek to channel human desire, Nordine's work celebrates mystery and possibility. He is filled with wonder at numbers, colors, words, chewing gum, rats in the basement, cracks in the ceiling, cement contractor stamps in sidewalks, backyard insects and birds and household pets, amazed by the strangeness of the ordinary and the familiar, awed by the incomprehensibility of time and mind. In the exploration of these themes, Nordine has brought into effective action a remarkable range of forms, including stories, plays, fables, vignettes, monologues, dialogues and "multiphrenic" exchanges, articulations of inner speech and free association, sketches, parables, musings and meditations, chants, songs, prose poems, free verse and rhymed verse, sound collages, soundscapes and sonic abstraction.

Ken Nordine's work remains, I suppose, situated somewhere at the outer edges of the periphery of American consciousness. Apart from serving as inspiration for poet-musician Tom Waits and composer-performance artist Laurie Anderson, his influence is unknowable. Clearly, though, purchasers sufficiently numerous bought and listened to those word jazz LPs and CDs, and more must have listened late nights to his radio shows. And I suspect that Nordine's wit and whimsy, his deft, dexterous imagination and independent cast of mind encouraged many in that unseen audience of solitary listeners to question standard cultural assumptions and consider alternate perspectives and wider paradigms.

A final word on word jazz: it is a considerable achievement and one that is likely to endure.

NOTES

[1] *Word Jazz* Dot records, DLP 3075. Recorded July 1957, released 1957.

[2] *Publication One (published impulsively)* by Ken Nordine. No date, no pagination. Ca. 1957.

[3] *Hard Bop* by David H. Rosenthal. N.Y. 1992, p. 77.

[4] *Blows Like a Horn* by Preston Whaley Jr. N.Y. 2004, p. 196.

[5] *Jazz Talk* by Robert S. Gold. N.Y. 1975, p. 222.

[6] *Lost Sound: The Forgotten Art of Radio Storytelling* by Jeff Porter. N.Y. 2016, p. 11.

[7] *The Art of Radio* by Donald McWhinnie. London: 1959, p. 25.

[8] *Spoken Word: Postwar American Phonograph Cultures* by Jacob Smith. N.Y. 2011, p. 45.

[9] *Ibid.*

[10] Others viewing Ken Nordine's *Word Jazz* as an expression of hip culture include: Stephen Ronan in *Discs of the Gone World* (1996); Phil Ford in "Hip Sensibility in an Age of Mass Counterculture," *Jazz Perspectives* Vol. 2, No. 2, November 2008, pp. 121-163; and Vwadek P. Marciniak in *Politics, Humor and the Counterculture* N.Y. 2008. See also: Bob Rolontz "Whatever Became of Jazz and Poetry?" in *The Jazz Word,* ed. by Dom Cerulli, Burt Korall & Mort Nasatir, N.Y. 1960, pp. 117-122.

[11] *Flappers 2 Rappers: American Youth Slang* by Tom Dalzell. Springfied, Mass: 1996, p. 57.

[12] *The Hip: Hipsters, Jazz and the Beat Generation* by Roy Carr, Brian Case & Fred Dellar. London: 1986, p. 11.

[13] "The Concept of Hipness: The Search for a Meaningful Definition" by Steven Brown Goldberg. *The Journal of Popular Culture,* Spring 1979, Vol. 2, No. 4, p. 617.

[14] "Hip Sensibility in an Age of Mass Counterculture" by Phil Ford. *Jazz Perspectives,* Vol. 2, No. 2, November 2008, pp. 121-163.

[15] *Ibid.* pp. 122-23.

[16] *Hip: The History* by John Leland, N.Y. 2004, p.69.

[17] *No Room for Squares: The Hip and Modern Image of Blue Note Records 1954-1967* by Alisa White. Thesis. Indiana State University, 2011, p. i. https://iucat.iu.edu./iun/ 1066841

[18] *Ibid.*

[19] *The Lonely Crowd* by David Riesman, N.Y. 1950; *The Organization Man* by William H. Whyte, N.Y. 1956; *The Man in the Gray Flannel Suit* by Sloan Wilson, N.Y. 1956.

[20] Porter, Jeff. *Op. Cit.* p. 204.

[21] Ford, Phil. *Op. Cit.* p. 144.

[22] *Son of Word Jazz,* Dot records, DLP 3096. Recorded 1957, released 1958.

[23] Proverbs 16:18. *King James Bible.*

[24] *Next,* Dot records, DLP 25196. Released 1959.

[25] *Collected Poems 1909-1962* by T.S. Eliot, London: 1963, p. 79.

[26] *The Holy Bible,* Daniel, 5.

[27] *Word Jazz Volume II,* Dot Records, DLP 25301. Released 1960.

[28] *The Autobiography of Benjamin Franklin* (1793). Novels by Horatio Alger include: *Ragged Dick* (1868), *Fame and Fortune* (1868), *Stuggling Upward* (1868) and *Luck and Pluck* (1869).

[29] *Arthur Rimbaud: Selected Poems and Letters,* translated by Jeremy Harding and John Sturrock. London: 2004, pp. 94-95.

[30] *Myths, Dreams and Mysteries* by Mircea Eliade. N.Y. 1960, pp. 59-60.

[31] *Essays in Zen Buddhism* by D.T. Suzuki. London: 1926, p. 24.

[32] *The Complete Poems and Plays* by T.S. Eliot. New York: 1952, p. 145.

[33] *Stare with your Ears,* Snail Records, SR 1001. Released 1979.

[34] *John Donne: Selected Writings* edited by Janel Mueller. Oxford: 2015, pp. 298-299.

[35] "The Syntax and Semantics of Personal Datives" by Corrine Hutchinson and Grant Armstrong, in *Microsyntactic Variation in North American English,* edited by Raffaella Zanuttini and Laurence R. Horn. Oxford: 2014, p. 189.

[36] *The American Dream* by Jim Cullen. Oxford: 2003, p. 165.

[37] *Epistle of St. Paul to the Philippians* 2:6-7.

[38] *Triple Talk,* Snail Records, 1984. Released as audio cassette only.

[39] *Lost Sound: The Forgotten Art of Radio Storytelling, op. cit.* pp. 204-05.

[40] The City of Destruction is the starting place for the protagonist, Christian, on his pilgrimage through dangerous and treacherous terrain to the Celestial City in John Bunyan's *The Pilgrim's Progress from This World to That Which Is to Come* (1678).

[41] *Devout Catalyst,* Grateful Dead Records, GDCD 40152. Released 1992.

[42] *A Transparent Mask,* Asphodel, ASP 2004. Released 2001.

[43] *Hamlet* by William Shakespeare, Act 5, Scene 2, lines 92-93. Hamlet's allusion is to *The New Testament*, Matthew 10:29.

[44] *Grandson of Word Jazz,* Snail Records, SR 1003. Released 1986.

[45] The Co-Existence Bagel Shop, located at 1398 Grant Avenue, San Franciscio. Beat Generation hangout owned by Jay Hoppe. *Abomunist Manifesto* by Bob Kaufman, San Francisco: City Lights Books, 1959. *The Happy Birthday of Death* by Gregory Corso, N.Y.: New Directions, 1960.

[46] *Bits and Pieces of Word Jazz,* Snail Records, released 2014.

[47] *The Zurau Aphorisms* by Franz Kafka, translated by Michael Hofmann, Schocken, N.J. 2006, p. 16. Aphorism No. 16: *Ein Käfig ging einen Vogel suchen.*

[48] "Will Ken Nordine Ever Grow Up?" by Adam Langer, *Chicago Reader:* www.chicagoreader.com/chicago/will-ken-nordine-ever-grow-up/Content?oid p. 5

[49] *The Eye is Never Filled: Word Jazz in Morphing Pictures,* Snail Records, released July 2005.